# 11+ & SATs MATHS

## Book One

Stephen C. Curran

edited by
Anne-Marie Choong
Tandip Singh Mann

**This book belongs to:**

.......................................................

Accelerated Education Publications Ltd.

# Contents



2

# Chapter One
# BASIC NUMBER
## 1. Tens Number System

The Tens Number System is also called the **Denary System**.

- Single figures are termed **Digits**.
- Groups of digits are termed **Numbers**.
- **Place Value** means that the position of a Digit in any number represents its value.

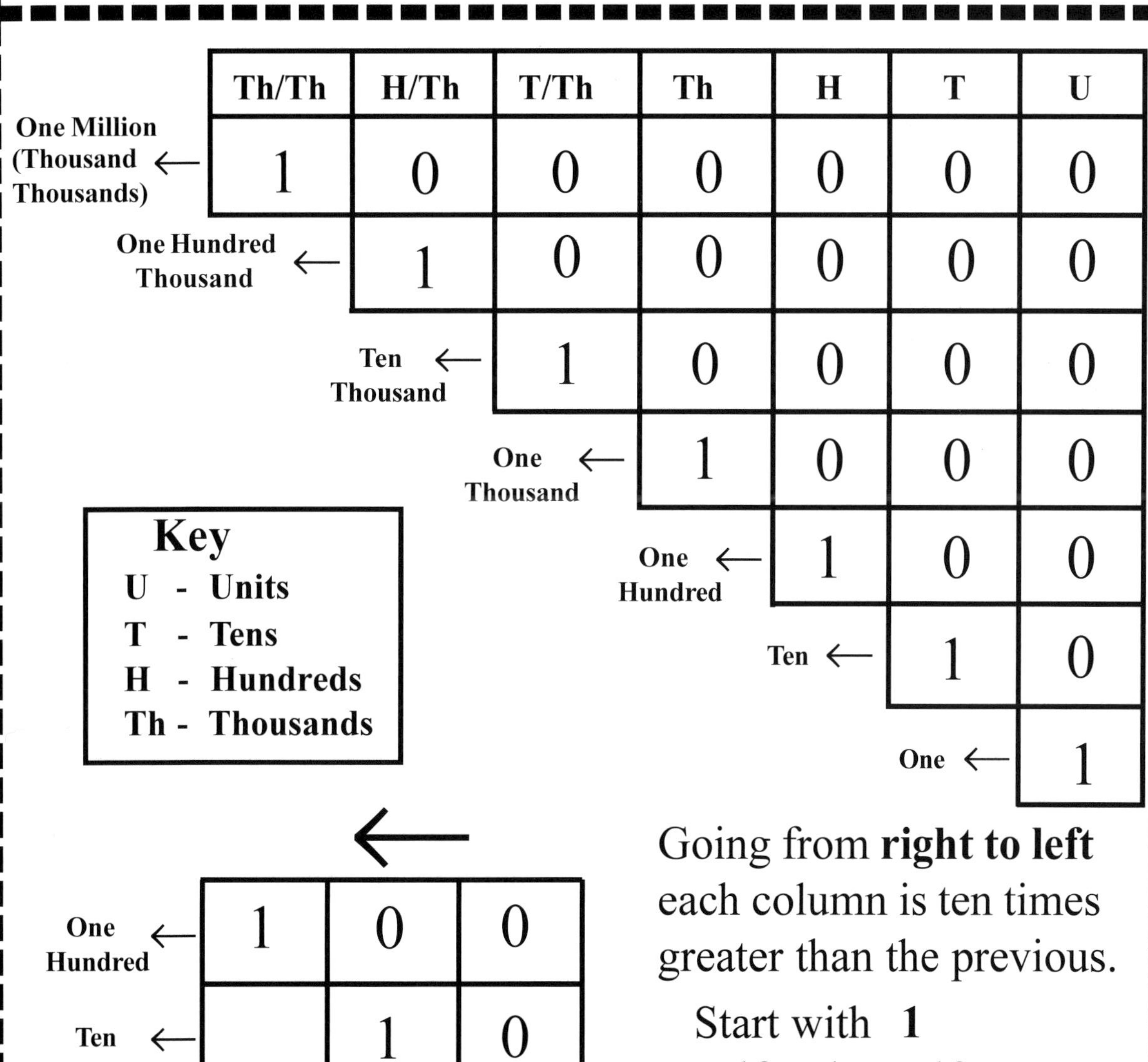

| | Th/Th | H/Th | T/Th | Th | H | T | U |
|---|---|---|---|---|---|---|---|
| One Million (Thousand Thousands) ← | 1 | 0 | 0 | 0 | 0 | 0 | 0 |
| One Hundred Thousand ← | | 1 | 0 | 0 | 0 | 0 | 0 |
| Ten Thousand ← | | | 1 | 0 | 0 | 0 | 0 |
| One Thousand ← | | | | 1 | 0 | 0 | 0 |
| One Hundred ← | | | | | 1 | 0 | 0 |
| Ten ← | | | | | | 1 | 0 |
| One ← | | | | | | | 1 |

**Key**

- U  - Units
- T  - Tens
- H  - Hundreds
- Th - Thousands

| | | |
|---|---|---|
| One Hundred ← | 1 | 0 | 0 |
| Ten ← | | 1 | 0 |
| One ← | | | 1 |

Going from **right to left** each column is ten times greater than the previous.

Start with  **1**

$$10 \times 1 = 10$$
$$10 \times 10 = 100$$
$$10 \times 100 = 1,000$$

# a. Numbers in Figures

Place the number in the table (Start in **100,000** column).
Example:

| Five hundred thousand and twenty three **in Figures** would be: | **500,023** |

---

## Exercise 1: 1

Write the numbers **in Figures**:

1)  Thirty five.                                =  ........................

2)  Four hundred and nine.                      =  ........................

3)  One hundred thousand.                       =  ........................

4)  Four hundred and forty six.                 =  ........................

5)  Six thousand and twenty one.                =  ........................

6)  Seventy five thousand.                      =  ........................

7)  Nine hundred and sixty five
    thousand.                                   =  ........................

8)  One million, four hundred
    thousand.                                   =  ........................

9)  Nine hundred and forty nine.                =  ........................

10) One hundred and fifty two
    thousand, three hundred and                 =  ........................
    ninety five.

**Score Out of Ten** →

# b. Numbers in Writing

Place the number in the table (Start in **1,000** column).

Example: | **7,093** in Words would be **written** as: |
'Seven thousand and ninety three'.

---

**Exercise 1: 2**   Put the Figures into **Writing**:

Score

1)   **11** = ........................   2)   **23** = ..............................
........................................

3)   **899** = ........................
............................................ 4)   **190** = ........................
........................................        ........................................

5)   **359** = ............................................................
............................................................

6)   **1,310** = ............................................................
............................................................

7)   **25,853** = ............................................................
............................................................

8)   **69,942** = ............................................................
............................................................

9)   **234,300** = ............................................................
............................................................

10)  **1,545,770** = ............................................................
............................................................
............................................................

# c. Number Values

## Exercise 1: 3    Calculate the following:

1) Rearrange these numbers in size order, highest first.

   **3,561**    **772**    **5,743**    **9,990**    **1,232**    **9,078**

   .........    ..........    ..........    ..........    ..........    ..........

   Write the value of the underlined Figures.

2) In **Writing**                    3) In **Numbers**

   **46,4<u>5</u>2**    **67<u>8</u>**          **33,<u>6</u>74**    **<u>55</u>**    **7<u>5</u>6, 394**

   ..........    ..........          ..........    .......    ...............

4) Which is More?                    5) Which is Less?

   **357,929**  or  **376,216**          **79,433**  or  **79,511**

   ...................          ...................

6) Write out all the numbers that can be made from **789** in size order, largest first (The first is done).

   987    .........    .........    .........    .........    .........

7) Which is Less?                    8) Which is More?

   **531,888  or  516,998**          **11,001**  or  **11,210**

   ...................          ...................

9) Rearrange these numbers in size order, lowest first.

   **1,192**    **88**    **8,754**    **901**    **12**    **7,069**

   .........    ..........    ..........    ..........    ..........    ..........

10) What is the smallest number that can be made from **58,193**?    ...................

Score

    

# 2. Addition

Example: $568 + 369$

$$
\begin{array}{r}
5\,6\,8 \\
3\,6\,9\, + \\
\hline
9\,3\,7 \\
\hline
1\ \ 1
\end{array}
$$

← Start here
$8 + 9 = 17$

Carry ten to next column.

---

## Exercise 1: 4a

1) 
$$
\begin{array}{r}
6\,6\,9\,2 \\
4\,8\,6\,1\, + \\
\hline
\end{array}
$$

2) 
$$
\begin{array}{r}
6\,2\,9\,3 \\
3\,1\,4\,8\, + \\
\hline
\end{array}
$$

3) 
$$
\begin{array}{r}
4\,5\,7\,1 \\
2\,1\,9\,7\, + \\
\hline
\end{array}
$$

4) 
$$
\begin{array}{r}
5\,1\,2\,3 \\
8\,4\,9\,9\, + \\
\hline
\end{array}
$$

---

### Addition Terms

- Add
- Plus
- Total
- Increase
- Enlarge
- Combine
- Find the Total of
- Find the Sum of

---

If numbers are missing. Example:

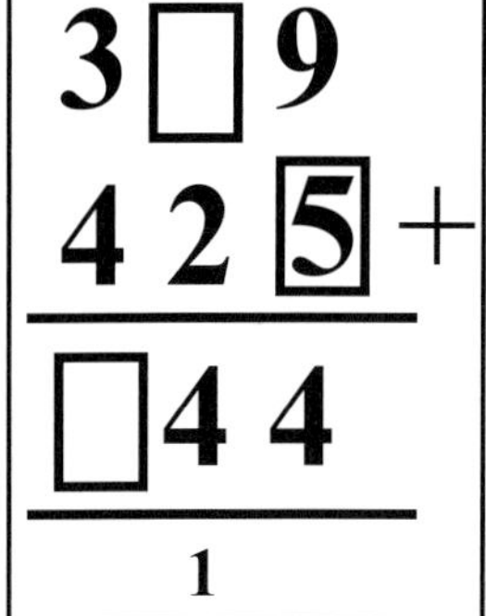

$9 + ? = 14$
Missing Number must be **5**.

Follow the normal stages of Addition.

---

## Exercise 1: 4b

Score

5) 
$$
\begin{array}{r}
\square\,8\,9 \\
8\,7\,\square\, + \\
\hline
1\,6\,\square\,4
\end{array}
$$

6) 
$$
\begin{array}{r}
6\,\square\,3 \\
7\,8\,5\, + \\
\hline
\square\,4\,6\,\square
\end{array}
$$

7) 
$$
\begin{array}{r}
6\,1\,\square\,3 \\
9\,7\,8\,0\, + \\
\hline
\square\,5\,\square\,0\,3
\end{array}
$$

8) 
$$
\begin{array}{r}
5\,0\,\square\,8 \\
7\,\square\,8\,0\, + \\
\hline
1\,3\,0\,5\,\square
\end{array}
$$

9) 
$$
\begin{array}{r}
\square\,5\,6\,7 \\
6\,7\,8\,\square\, + \\
\hline
1\,1\,\square\,5\,3
\end{array}
$$

10) 
$$
\begin{array}{r}
\square\,8\,7\,\square \\
9\,7\,3\,1\, + \\
\hline
1\,1\,6\,\square\,6
\end{array}
$$

# 3. Subtraction

## a. Method One

The **standard method** involves **Borrowing from the top**.

$$\begin{array}{r} {}^{4}\cancel{5}\,{}^{13}\cancel{4}\,{}^{1}2 \\ 7\,9\, - \\ \hline 4\,6\,3 \\ \hline \end{array}$$

Example: $\boxed{542 - 79}$

2 − 9 we cannot do.
Borrow ten from 40.
Cross out 4 and make it 3.
2 becomes 12 (10 + 2) then Subtract.
Continue same method to the end.

---

### Exercise 1: 5a

1) $\begin{array}{r} 6\,4\,7\,8 \\ 4\,2\,4\,5\, - \\ \hline \end{array}$
2) $\begin{array}{r} 8\,6\,7\,9 \\ 9\,1\,2\, - \\ \hline \end{array}$

3) $\begin{array}{r} 6\,8\,3\,6 \\ 5\,4\,9\,8\, - \\ \hline \end{array}$
4) $\begin{array}{r} 6\,7\,1\,0 \\ 8\,9\,5\, - \\ \hline \end{array}$

**Subtraction Terms**
- Subtract
- Less
- Minus
- Take away/from
- Deduct
- Decrease
- Reduce
- Find the difference

---

Example:

$\boxed{300 - 164}$

$$\begin{array}{r} {}^{2}\cancel{3}\,{}^{9}\cancel{0}\,{}^{1}0 \\ 1\,6\,4\, - \\ \hline 1\,3\,6 \\ \hline \end{array}$$

What if there are zeros at the top?

0 − 4 we cannot do.
We can't borrow from the tens
column, but can from the hundreds.
Take 100 from 300, leaving 200.
Cross out 3, make it 2.
Use the 100 to fill up tens & units column.
90 in the tens - cross out zero, write 9.
10 in the units - write 1 (making 10).

## Exercise 1: 5b — Subtract the following:

5)  400
    237 −
    ____

    ____

6)  700
    513 −
    ____

    ____

7)  2000
    479 −
    ____

    ____

8)  6005
    4478 −
    ____

    ____

9)  4700
    1899 −
    ____

    ____

10) 7001
    4495 −
    ____

    ____

# b. Method Two

Method Two involves **Adding to the bottom**.

$$\begin{array}{r} {}^0\cancel{1}\,{}^1 0\,{}^1 0\,{}^1 0 \\ {}^6\cancel{5}\,{}^5\cancel{4}\,9\ - \\ \hline 4\,5\,1 \end{array}$$

Example: $\boxed{1000 - 549}$

$0 - 9$ we cannot do.
Borrow 10 and pay back.
· make 0 into 10.
· add 1 to 4 making 5.
Continue method to end of sum.

## Exercise 1: 6 — Subtract the following:

1)  1000
    678 −
    ____

    ____

2)  1000
    912 −
    ____

    ____

3)  1000
    792 −
    ____

    ____

4)  3000
    629 −
    ____

    ____

5)  2060
    787 −
    ____

    ____

6)  6100
    4699 −
    ____

    ____

7)  5010
    2256 −
    ____

    ____

8)  7001
    519 −
    ____

    ____

9)  42080
    10692 −
    ______

    ______

10) 30000
    1987 −
    ______

    ______

Score

**Missing Numbers** are found using Methods 1 and 2.

Example:

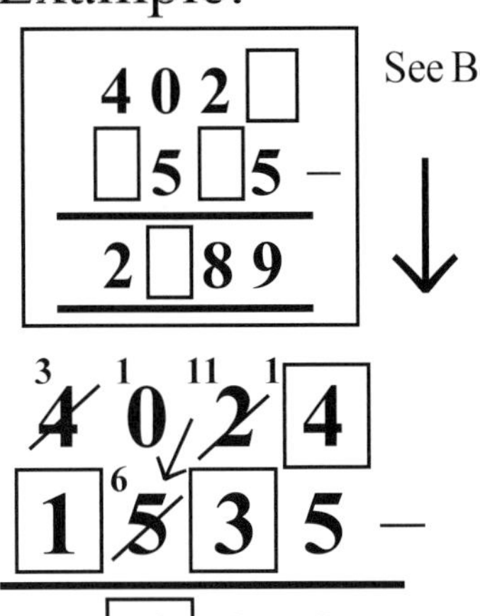

See Below ↓

$\boxed{?} - 5 = 9$ (Missing number is **4**).
Make the 2 in next column into 1.
Borrow 1, making 11.
$11 - \boxed{?} = 8$ (Missing number is **3**).
Pay back 1; make the 5 into 6.
Borrow 1, making 10.
Make 4 in the next column into 3.
$10 - 6 = \boxed{?}$ (Missing number is **4**).
$3 - \boxed{?} = 2$ (Missing number is **1**).

---

## Exercise 1: 7   Subtract the following:

1)
```
  7 □ 3
□ 3 □  −
───────
  5 5 2
```

2)
```
□ 0 5
3 □ 9  −
───────
1 7 □
```

3)
```
8 □ 0
1 1 □  −
───────
□ 8 7
```

4)
```
□ 9 1
2 □ 6  −
───────
2 9 □
```

5)
```
6 0 2 □
4 □ 6 2  −
─────────
□ 9 □ 2
```

6)
```
8 □ 1 4
□ 1 7 □  −
─────────
5 0 □ 5
```

7)
```
4 □ 0 □
2 9 □ 5  −
─────────
□ 8 8 9
```

8)
```
9 □ 3 8
□ 1 □ 3  −
─────────
6 9 9 □
```

9)
```
□ 0 □ 8
1 7 8 □  −
─────────
1 □ 1 9
```

10)
```
□ 1 0 □
3 □ 2 8  −
─────────
4 0 □ 9
```

**Score** □

# 4. Multiplication
## a. Short Multiplication

Use this method when Multiplying by single digits (1 - 9).

$$759 \times 9$$

$$
\begin{array}{r}
7\,5\,9 \\
9\, \times \\
\hline
6\,8\,3\,1 \\
\end{array}
$$

Example: $\boxed{759 \times 9}$

$9 \times 9 = 81$   Carry 8 and write **1**.
$9 \times 5 = 45$   Add 8   $45 + 8 = 53$.
Carry 5 and write **3**   $9 \times 7 = 63$.
Add 5   $63 + 5 = \mathbf{68}$

---

## Exercise 1: 8a   Multiply the following:   Score

1)  6 9 3 2
       3 ×

2)  5 4 9 7
       4 ×

3)  5 9 8 7
       5 ×

4)  7 9 5 1
       6 ×

5)  7 5 2 0
       7 ×

6)  9 8 6 1
       8 ×

---

Finding Missing Numbers.
Example:

$$
\begin{array}{r}
9\,5\,\square \\
4\, \times \\
\hline
\square\,8\,2\,0 \\
\end{array}
$$

$4 \times ? = ?0$
It must be
$4 \times \mathbf{5} = 20$

$$
\begin{array}{r}
9\,5\,\boxed{5} \\
4\, \times \\
\hline
\boxed{3}\,8\,2\,0 \\
\end{array}
$$

Do as a
Normal
Multiply

## Exercise 1: 8b

7)  8 9 2
     $\square$ ×
    $\square$ 7 8 4

8)  7 6 $\square$
       3 ×
    2 $\square$ 0 4

9)  9 $\square$ 6
       8 ×
    7 $\square$ 0 8

10)  $\square$ 0 8
        9 ×
     8 1 7 $\square$

- The number being Multiplied is the **Multiplicand**.
- The number we Multiply by is the **Multiplier**.
- The number we obtain is the **Product**.

$$
\begin{array}{r}
3\,7 \quad \leftarrow \text{Multiplicand}\\
4\,\times \quad \leftarrow \text{Multiplier}\\
\hline
1\,4\,8 \quad \leftarrow \text{Product}\\
\end{array}
$$

# b. Multiplying by Tens

To Multiply by **10** we add a **0**.　　$2 \times 10 = 20$

To Multiply by **100** we add **00**.　　$2 \times 100 = 200$

To Multiply by **1,000** we add **000**.　　$2 \times 1,000 = 2,000$

Example: $\boxed{100 \times 2,000}$

Just count the number of zeros on the Multiplier and add the same number of zeros on the Muliplicand.

$$100 \times 2,000 = 200,000$$

## Exercise 1: 9　Multiply the following:　Score ☐

1)  $5 \times 10 =$ ..............　　2)  $6 \times 100 =$ ..............

3)  $7 \times 1,000 =$ ..............　　4)  $25 \times 100 =$ ..............

5)  $10 \times 30 =$ ..............　　6)  $100 \times 100 =$ ..............

7)  $100 \times 150 =$ ..............　　8)  $1,000 \times 55 =$ ..............

9)  $100 \times 13 =$ ..............　　10)  $10 \times 5,000 =$ ..............

# c. Long Multiplication

This is used when Multiplying by more than 1 digit.
**Method 1** - This involves breaking the sum into two distinct parts. Example: | Multiply **213** by **23** |

1. Multiply 213 by the 3 units as in short Division.

$$
\begin{array}{r}
2\,1\,3 \\
3\times \\
\hline
6\,3\,9
\end{array}
$$

2. Multiply the 20 units (two tens). Place a zero in the first space as the units have been Multiplied already.

$$
\begin{array}{r}
2\,1\,3 \\
2\,0\times \\
\hline
4\,2\,6\,0
\end{array}
$$

3. Add the two results together to attain the answer.

$$
\begin{array}{r}
6\,3\,9 \\
4\,2\,6\,0+ \\
\hline
4\,8\,9\,9
\end{array}
$$

---

## Exercise 1: 10   Multiply the following:   Score

1) Multiply **35** by **23**.

$$
\begin{array}{r}
3\,5 \\
3\times \\
\hline
\end{array}
\qquad
\begin{array}{r}
3\,5 \\
2\,0\times \\
\hline
0
\end{array}
$$

$$+$$

Add the two sums to find the answer ........................

2) Multiply **97** by **45**.

$$
\begin{array}{r}
9\,7 \\
5\times \\
\hline
\end{array}
\qquad
\begin{array}{r}
9\,7 \\
4\,0\times \\
\hline
0
\end{array}
$$

$$+$$

Add the two sums to find the answer ........................

3) Multiply **57** by **19**.

| 5 7 | 5 7 |
|---|---|
| 9 × | 1 0 × |
| | + 0 |

Answer ......................

4) Multiply **43** by **25**.

| 4 3 | 4 3 |
|---|---|
| 5 × | 2 0 × |
| | + 0 |

Answer ......................

5) Multiply **355** by **34**.

| 3 5 5 | 3 5 5 |
|---|---|
| 4 × | 3 0 × |
| | + 0 |

Answer ......................

6) Multiply **267** by **24**.

| 2 6 7 | 2 6 7 |
|---|---|
| 4 × | 2 0 × |
| | + 0 |

Answer ......................

7) Multiply **475** by **78**.

| 4 7 5 | 4 7 5 |
|---|---|
| 8 × | 7 0 × |
| | + 0 |

Answer ......................

8) Multiply **547** by **32**.

| 5 4 7 | 5 4 7 |
|---|---|
| 2 × | 3 0 × |
| | + 0 |

Answer ......................

9) Multiply **1534** by **68**.

| 1 5 3 4 | 1 5 3 4 |
|---|---|
| 8 × | 6 0 × |
| | + 0 |

Answer ......................

10) Multiply **2825** by **57**.

| 2 8 2 5 | 2 8 2 5 |
|---|---|
| 7 × | 5 0 × |
| | + 0 |

Answer ......................

<u>**Method 2**</u> - The **Italian Method** combines both sums and can also be used when Multiplying by more than 1 digit.

Example: | Multiply **213** by **23** |

Ignore the 2 and Multiply by 3.
Line 1 - 3 × 213 = 639.
Now Multiply by 2  (See arrows).
Line 2 - Put a 0 in units column.
     - 20 × 213 = 4260.
Add Line 1 and Line 2  =  Line 3.
639 + 4260 = 4899

```
    2 1 3
    2 3 ×
  ───────
    6 3 9    Line 1
  ---------
 +4 2 6 0    Line 2
  ───────
  4 8 9 9    Line 3
```

# Exercise 1: 11   Multiply the following:   Score

1)   3 4
    1 8 ×
-----------
      0

2)   7 3
    4 2 ×
-----------
      0

3)   6 2
    4 3 ×
-----------
      0

4)   5 6
    2 6 ×
-----------
      0

5)   8 2 8
    9 3 ×

6)   7 1 9
    9 2 ×

7)   2 4 5
    4 5 ×

8)   5 3 4 9
    4 3 ×

9)   6 9 8 7
    5 8 ×

10)   8 3 9 7
    7 6 ×



15

# 5. Division
## a. Short Division

This method is used when Dividing by a single Digit.

Example: $625 \div 8$

8 Divides 62 **seven** times, Remainder 6.
Write 7 and carry the 6.
8 Divides 65 **eight** times, Remainder 1.
Write 8 and put a Remainder of **1**.

$$7\,8 \text{ Rem. 1}$$
$$8\,|\,6\,2\,^6 5$$

## Exercise 1: 12a (Questions 1-3 have no Remainders.)

1) $8\,|\,6\,8\,8$    2) $4\,|\,3\,7\,6$    3) $6\,|\,5\,8\,8$

(Questions 4-6 have Remainders.)

4) $3\,|\,4\,8\,9\,5$    5) $7\,|\,6\,9\,2\,6$    6) $9\,|\,8\,7\,4\,5\,4$

Example:   If numbers are missing do the following:

$$1\,\square\,9 \text{ Rem. 3}$$
$$6\,|\,8\,^2 9\,^5 7$$
$$\rightarrow$$
$$1\,4\,9 \text{ Rem. 3}$$
$$6\,|\,8\,^2 9\,^5 7$$

The missing number must be **4**.

## Exercise 1: 12b  Fill in the missing numbers:

Score

$$4\,\square\,6$$
7) $7\,|\,2\,9\,8\,2$

$$\square\,9\,5$$
8) $9\,|\,3\,5\,5\,5$

$$8\,1\,8$$
9) $8\,|\,6\,5\,4\,\square$

$$2\,0\,2$$
10) $7\,|\,1\,\square\,1\,4$

**Division Terms**
- Share
- Divide
- Find the Quotient
- Partition

To find:
- A Half (Divide by **2**)
- A Third (Divide by **3**)
- A Quarter/Fourth (Divide by **4**)
- A Fifth (Divide by **5**)

We Divide by the **Divisor or Divider**.
We Divide into the **Dividend**.
We obtain the **Quotient**.
The left over is **a Remainder**.

$$\text{Quotient} \searrow \quad \underset{\text{Divisor} \rightarrow}{} 4\,\overline{)6\,{}^2 5} \quad 1\,6_{\,r.\,1} \nwarrow \text{Remainder}$$

Quotient → 1 6 r.1 ← Remainder
Divisor → 4 ⟌ 6²5 ← Dividend

# b. Dividing by Tens

To Divide by **10** we remove a **0**.     $20 \div 10 = 2$
To Divide by a **100** we remove **00**.     $200 \div 100 = 2$
To Divide by **1,000** we remove **000**.   $2,000 \div 1,000 = 2$

Example: $\boxed{4,000 \div 100}$

Just count the number of zeros on the Divisor and remove the same number of zeros from the Dividend.

$$4,000 \div 100 = 40$$

## Exercise 1: 13   Divide the following:     Score ☐

1) $50 \div 10 = $ .............

2) $300 \div 100 = $ .............

3) $5,000 \div 100 = $ .............

4) $560 \div 10 = $ .............

5) $200 \div 100 = $ .............

6) $3,200 \div 10 = $ .............

7) $400 \div 10 = $ .............

8) $520 \div 10 = $ .............

9) $6,000 \div 100 = $ .............

10) $5,900 \div 100 = $ .............

# c. Long Division

This method is used when Dividing by two digits.

Example: $4926 \div 24$

$$24 \overline{)4926} = 205 \text{ r.}6$$

Subtract to find the Remainders

Rough Work

Guess and Test

| 24 | 24 |
|---|---|
| $4\times$ | $5\times$ |
| 96 | 120 |

Only up to $9\times$ per number

24 can't Divide 4 into whole numbers.
24 Divides 49 twice.
Write **2** in the answer.
$2 \times 24 = 48$
Write 48 under 49.
**Subtract** $49 - 48 = 1$.
Bring down the 2.
24 will not Divide 12.
Put a **zero** in the answer.
Bring down the 6.
24 Divides 126 by 5 (rough work).
Write **5** in the answer.
$5 \times 24 = 120$
Write 120 under 126 and **Subtract.**
24 will not Divide 6.
There is a Remainder of **6.**

To help you divide use
<u>D</u>addy
<u>M</u>ummy
<u>S</u>ister
<u>B</u>rother
(D - Divide)
(M - Multiply)
(S - Subtract)
(B - Bring Down)

In Long Division Remainders are found by **Subtracting on paper** instead of using mental calculations (the only difference between Long and Short Division).

## Exercise 1: 14    (Questions 1- 4 have no Remainders.)

1) $14 \overline{)9156}$    2) $13 \overline{)8957}$

= ..............    = ..............

3) $17\overline{)5457}$     4) $19\overline{)7828}$

= ...............

= ...............

5) $18\overline{)4885}$     6) $21\overline{)6328}$

= ...............

= ...............

7) $16\overline{)10939}$     8) $15\overline{)14051}$

= ...............

= ...............

9) $23\overline{)13375}$     10) $25\overline{)23854}$

= ...............

= ...............

**Score**

# 6. Words to Number Problems

Questions can involve changing Words into one or more of the **Four Rules of Number**.

$$+ \quad - \quad \times \quad \div$$

Remind yourself of the terms: **Addition; Subtraction; Multiplication; Division**

Example: Add the Product of **10** and **12** to the Sum of **10** and **12** and the Difference between **10** and **12**.

Look for the **Starting Point**. It is necessary to do each separate Sum before Adding up all the answers.

1. The Product of **10** and **12**.  $10 \times 12 = 120$
2. The Sum of **10** and **12**.  $10 + 12 = 22$
3. The Difference between **10** and **12**.  $12 - 10 = 2 +$

Now Add up the answers to the three Parts:  $\underline{144}$

---

## Exercise 1: 15   Answer the following:   Score

1) What is the Sum of the Numbers here that are Divisible by **5**? ............   **36, 75, 162, 460, 545**

2) Find the Difference between the Quotient of **12** and **4** and the Product of **12** and **4** .............

3) Find the Sum of the of first ten numbers (**1** to **10**) ............

4) How many times can **27** be Subtracted from **1242**? ............

5) Deduct **23** from **60**, then Add **15** ..........

6) Double **16** and then Reduce it by **13** ..........

7) Treble **31** and Take Away **19** ..........

8) Halve **28** and Add **4**. Then Multiply this by **3** ..........

9) Decrease **11** by **5** and Divide by **3** ..........

10) Quadruple **8** and Subtract **4**. Divide this by **7** ..........

# 7. Inverse Operations

It is useful to understand the relationship between the Four Rules of Number. **Inverse means Opposite.**

$+$ and $-$ are a pair of Inverse Operations.

$5 + 4 = 9$ ;    $9 - 4 = 5$ ;    $9 - 5 = 4$

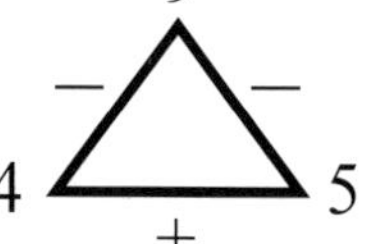

$\times$ and $\div$ are a pair of Inverse Operations.

$3 \times 4 = 12$ ;    $12 \div 4 = 3$ ;    $12 \div 3 = 4$

---

Example:

| Show Adding & Subtracting are Inverse Operations. |

$$\begin{array}{r} 5\,3 \\ 4\,2\,+ \\ \hline 9\,5 \end{array} \qquad \begin{array}{r} 9\,5 \\ 4\,2\,- \\ \hline 5\,3 \end{array} \qquad \begin{array}{r} 9\,5 \\ 5\,3\,- \\ \hline 4\,2 \end{array}$$

$53 + 42 = 95$ | $95 - 42 = 53$
$95 - 53 = 42$

Example:

| Show Multiplying & Dividing are Inverse Operations. |

$$\begin{array}{r} 1\,2 \\ 6\,\times \\ \hline 7\,2 \end{array} \qquad 12\overline{)72}^{\;6} \qquad 6\overline{)72}^{\;1\,2}$$

$6 \times 12 = 72$ | $72 \div 12 = 6$
$72 \div 6 = 12$

---

## Exercise 1: 16  Calculate the following:    **Score** ☐

1-2)
$$\begin{array}{r} 5\,5 \\ 6\,4\,+ \\ \hline \Box \end{array} \qquad \begin{array}{r} 1\,1\,9 \\ \Box\,- \\ \hline 5\,5 \end{array}$$

3-5)
$$\begin{array}{r} 7\,9 \\ \Box\,+ \\ \hline 1\,2\,7 \end{array} \qquad \begin{array}{r} \Box \\ 4\,8\,- \\ \hline 7\,9 \end{array} \qquad \begin{array}{r} 1\,2\,7 \\ \Box\,- \\ \hline 4\,8 \end{array}$$

6-7)
$$\begin{array}{r} 4\,3 \\ 3\,4\,\times \end{array}$$

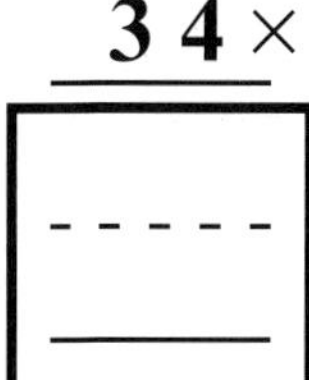

$34\overline{)1462}$

8-10)
$$\begin{array}{r} 2\,7 \\ 4\,8\,\times \end{array}$$

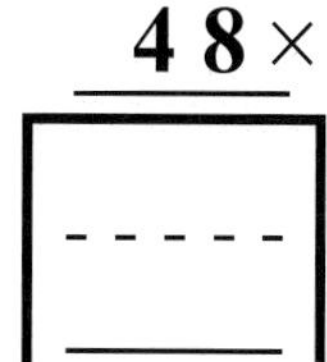

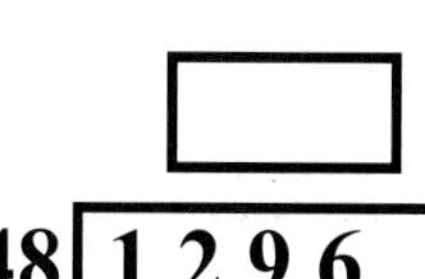

$27\overline{)1296}$

$48\overline{)1296}$

# 8. Inverse Problems

**All Inverse Problems are solved by reversing the Operations:**

| Add $\longleftrightarrow$ Subtract | Multiply $\longleftrightarrow$ Divide |

## a. The Forwards Type

The information in these questions can be dealt with in the order it is given. i.e. in a 'Forwards' fashion.

Example: **24 is 8 more than half this number.**

**Start here** $\textbf{24}$ is **8** more than **half** this number.
$- 8$ (8 less)  $\times 2$ (2 times)

The Sum can be written as: $(24 - 8) \times 2 = 32$

---

### Exercise 1: 17a    Answer the following:

1) **14** is **6 more** than a **quarter** of this number ..........

2) **35** is **7 less** than **six times** this number ..........

3) **17** is **10 more** than a **third** of this number ..........

4) **12** is **14 less** than a **fifth** of this number ..........

5) **24** is **4 more** than **five times** this number ..........

## b. The Backwards Type

The information in these questions is dealt with in reverse order. i.e. in a 'Backwards' fashion.

Example: **If we Add 9 and Subtract 4 the answer is 20.**

$- 9$ (Subtract 9)    $+ 4$ (Add 4) $\longleftarrow$ **Start here**

If we **Add 9** and **Subtract 4** the answer is $\textbf{20}$

The Sum can be written as: $(20 + 4) - 9 = 15$

Score

## Exercise 1: 17b  Answer the following:

6) If we **Add 12** and **Subtract 5** the answer is **50** ..........
7) If we **Double it** and **Subtract 6** the answer is **24** ..........
8) If we **Subtract 5** and **Add 15** the answer is **63** ..........
9) If we **Treble it** and **Add 9** the answer is **72** ..........
10) If we **Add 16** and then **Divide by 3** the answer is **51** .........

## c. Smaller-Larger Type (Add/Subtract)

The Inverse Operation is indicated by 'Smaller' or 'Larger'.
If it says it is **Smaller** - make it **Larger** - **Add**.
If it says it is **Larger** - make it **Smaller** - **Subtract**.

Example: | 9 is **Smaller** than this number by **15**. |

It says it is **Smaller** so we make it **Larger** and **Add**.
The Sum can be written as:  $9 + 15 = 24$

## Exercise 1: 18a    Answer the following:

1) **14** is Larger than this number by **9** ..........
2) **30** is Smaller than this number by **18** ..........
3) **97** is Larger than this number by **43** ..........
4) **125** is Smaller than this number by **64** ..........
5) **224** is Larger than this number by **83** ..........

## d. Smaller-Larger Type (Multiply/Divide)

The Inverse Operation in these questions is still indicated by
the words 'Smaller' or 'Larger'. However, if the word
'**Times**' is included it is a Multiply or Divide Type.
**Smaller** and **Times** means make it **Larger** - **Multiply**.
**Larger** and **Times** means make it **Smaller** - **Divide**.

## Exercise 1: 18b   Answer the following:

6) **250** is **5 Times Larger** than this number ..........

7) **12** is **8 Times Smaller** than this number ..........

8) **216** is **9 Times Larger** than this number ..........

9) **5** is **7 Times Smaller** than this number ..........

10) **56** is **7 Times Larger** than this number ..........

**Score**

# 9. More Number Problems

## Exercise 1: 19   Answer the following:   **Score**

1)
```
  □ 2 8 0
  5 3 □ 8 -
  ─────────
  1 □ 8 □
```

2) $32\overline{)5543}$

3) $560 \times 10,000 =$  ......................

4)
```
  2 5 4 3
      6 8 ×
  ─────────
  ─────────
```

5) Add **23** to **41**, then Subtract **8**. Divide by **4** .........

6) **13** is **14 Times Smaller** than this number. .........

7)
```
  4 0 1 3
  3 8 4 6 -
  ─────────
```

8)
```
  7 6 8 9
  7 9 7 6 +
  ─────────
```

9) **19** is **11 Less** than **one third** of this number. ............

10) What Number when Divided by **12** has an answer of **11** remainder **7**? (Clue - Multiply/Add) ......................

# Chapter Two
# NUMBER RELATIONSHIPS
## 1. Magic Squares

Magic Squares add up to the same amount horizontally, vertically and sometimes diagonally as well.

Example:

Find the Value of **A** in this Magic Square. It adds horizontally and vertically to **20** (not diagonally).

| 10 |    | 8 |
|----|----|---|
| A  |    | 9 |
|    | 11 |   |

**To find A**
Start with 8 and 9.
$8 + 9 = 17$
$20 - 17 = 3$

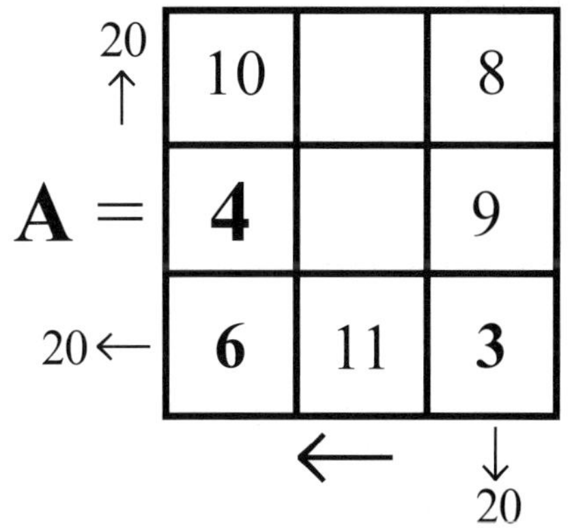


Completing the square.
$11 + 3 = 14$
$20 - 14 = 6$
$10 + 6 = 16$
$20 - 16 = 4$

$$A = 4$$

**Note: Always check rows and columns first, then diagonals.**

---

## Exercise 2: 1   Find the Missing Amounts:

1)   A = ..........

| 8  |   | 12 |
|----|---|----|
| A  |   |    |
|    | 3 | 14 |

Adds up to **31** vertically and horizontally only.

2)   A = ..........

| 9  |   | 9 |
|----|---|---|
| 16 | A |   |
|    |   | 15 |

Adds up to **28** vertically and horizontally only.

3-4)

A =

..........

B =

..........

| A | | 18 |
| B | | |
| 16 | 20 | 15 |

Adds up to **51** in all directions.

5-6)

A =

..........

B =

..........

| 15 | 20 | 13 |
| 14 | | B |
| | A | |

Adds up to **48** in all directions.

7-8)

A =

..........

B =

..........

| 12 | 8 | 13 |
| | 11 | |
| B | | A |

Adds up to **33** in all directions.

9-10)

A =

..........

B =

..........

| 50 | | 90 |
| 100 | | A |
| 30 | B | |

Adds up to **180** in all directions.

**Score**

# 2. Addition Squares

Addition Squares have two sections. The Sums section is grey (numbers to be Added) and the Answers section is white (answers to Addition sums).

Example:

Find the missing numbers.

| + | 7 | ? |
| 4 | 11 | 10 |
| 3 | ? | 9 |

There are **two missing numbers** in this Addition square.

| + | 7 | ? |
| 4 | 11 | 10 |
| 3 | **10** | 9 |

(**Add** the horizontal and vertical numbers to find an Addition answer - white squares.)

$$3 + 7 = \mathbf{10}$$

| + | 7 | 6 |
| 4 | 11 | 10 |
| 3 | **10** | 9 |

(Reverse the operation to **Minus** to find a number to be Added - grey squares.)

$$10 - 4 = \mathbf{6}$$

# Exercise 2: 2  Find the Missing Amounts:  Score

**1-2)**

A = ..........

B = ..........

| + | 4 | 9 |
|---|----|----|
| 6 | **A** | 15 |
| 8 | 12 | **B** |

**3-4)**

A = ..........

B = ..........

| + | 13 | 11 |
|---|----|----|
| **A** | 18 | 16 |
| **B** | 17 | 15 |

**5-7)**

A = ..........

B = ..........

C = ..........

| + | **A** | **B** |
|----|----|----|
| 11 | 18 | 21 |
| 13 | **C** | 23 |

**8-10)**

A = ..........

B = ..........

C = ..........

| + | 4 | 13 |
|----|----|----|
| **A** | 10 | 19 |
| **B** | 12 | **C** |

# 3. Subtraction Squares

Subtraction Squares work the opposite way to Addition Squares. The sums section is grey (numbers to be Subtracted) and the answers section is white (answers to Subtraction sums).

Example:

Find the missing numbers.

| − | 15 | ? |
|---|----|----|
| 9 | 6 | 13 |
| 2 | ? | 20 |

There are **two missing numbers** in this Subtraction Square.

| − | 15 | ? |
|---|----|----|
| 9 | 6 | 13 |
| 2 | **13** | 20 |

(**Subtract** the horizontal and vertical numbers to find a Subtraction answer - white squares.)

$$15 - 2 = \mathbf{13}$$

| − | 15 | **22** |
|---|----|----|
| 9 | 6 | 13 |
| 2 | **13** | 20 |

(Reverse the operation to **Add** to find a number to be Subtracted - grey squares.)

$$9 + 13 = \mathbf{22}$$

**1-2)**

A = ..........

B = ..........

| − | 11 | 14 |
|---|----|----|
| 7 | A | 7 |
| 3 | 8 | B |

**3-4)**

A = ..........

B = ..........

| − | 10 | 17 |
|---|----|----|
| A | 5 | 12 |
| B | 7 | 14 |

**5-7)**

A = ..........

B = ..........

C = ..........

| − | A | B |
|---|---|----|
| 5 | 7 | 16 |
| 12 | C | 9 |

**8-10)**

A = ..........

B = ..........

C = ..........

| − | 10 | 15 |
|---|---|----|
| A | 5 | 10 |
| B | 1 | C |

# 4. Multiplication Squares

Multiplication Squares have two sections. The Sums section is grey (numbers to be Multiplied) and the Answers section is white (answers to Multiplication Sums).
Example:

**Find the missing numbers.**

| × | 3 | 7 | 6 |
|---|----|----|----|
| 4 | 12 | 28 | 24 |
| 6 | 18 | ? | 36 |
| ? | 24 | 56 | 48 |

| × | 3 | 7 | 6 |
|---|----|----|----|
| 4 | 12 | 28 | 24 |
| 6 | 18 | **42** | 36 |
| **8** | 24 | 56 | 48 |

(**Multiply** the horizontal and vertical numbers to find an Answer - white squares.)

$6 \times 7 = \mathbf{42}$

(Reverse the operation to **Division** to find a Multiplier for one of the Sums - grey squares.)

$24 \div 3 = \mathbf{8}$

# Exercise 2: 4   Find the Missing Amounts:   Score [ ]

**1-2)**

A = ..........

B = ..........

| × | 7 | 6 | 3 |
|---|---|---|---|
| 2 | 14 | 12 | 6 |
| 5 | 35 | A | 15 |
| B | 70 | 60 | 30 |

**3-4)**

A = ..........

B = ..........

| × | 2 | 5 | 9 |
|---|---|---|---|
| 9 | 18 | 45 | A |
| B | 8 | 20 | 36 |
| 8 | 16 | 40 | 72 |

**5-7)**

A = ..........

B = ..........

C = ..........

| × | 5 | 2 | A |
|---|---|---|---|
| 7 | B | 14 | 49 |
| 9 | 45 | 18 | 63 |
| 3 | 15 | C | 21 |

**8-10)**

A = ..........

B = ..........

C = ..........

| × | A | 7 | 6 |
|---|---|---|---|
| 4 | 12 | B | 24 |
| 8 | 24 | 56 | 48 |
| C | 18 | 42 | 36 |

# 5. Division Squares

Division Squares work the opposite way to Multiplication Squares. The sums section is grey (numbers to be Divided) and the answers section is white (answers to Division sums). Example:

Find the missing numbers.

| ÷ | ? | 36 | 24 |
|---|---|---|---|
| 6 | 2 | 6 | 4 |
| 2 | 6 | ? | 12 |
| 3 | 4 | 12 | 8 |

| ÷ | 12 | 36 | 24 |
|---|---|---|---|
| 6 | 2 | 6 | 4 |
| 2 | 6 | **18** | 12 |
| 3 | 4 | 12 | 8 |

(**Divide** the horizontal and vertical numbers to find an answer - white squares.)

(Reverse the operation to **Multiplication** to find a Dividend for one of the sums - grey squares.)

$$36 \div 2 = \mathbf{18}$$

$$3 \times 4 = \mathbf{12}$$

**1-2)**

A = .........

B = .........

| ÷ | 6 | 12 | 36 |
|---|---|----|----|
| 6 | 1 | 2 | 6 |
| 2 | 3 | A | 18 |
| B | 2 | 4 | 12 |

**3-4)**

A = .........

B = .........

| ÷ | 30 | 20 | 60 |
|---|----|----|----|
| 5 | 6 | 4 | A |
| B | 15 | 10 | 30 |
| 10 | 3 | 2 | 6 |

**5-7)**

A = .........

B = .........

C = .........

| ÷ | 24 | 36 | A |
|---|----|----|---|
| 6 | B | 6 | 12 |
| 4 | 6 | 9 | 18 |
| 3 | 8 | C | 24 |

**8-10)**

A = .........

B = .........

C = .........

| ÷ | A | 90 | 135 |
|---|---|----|-----|
| 5 | 9 | B | 27 |
| 3 | 15 | 30 | 45 |
| C | 5 | 10 | 15 |

# 6. Chinese Multiplication

Chinese Multiplication is another way of Multiplying. It is also called 'Napier's Bones' or Lattice Multiplication.

Example: Multiply **169** by **45**.

### Stage 1

Draw a box 3 squares by 2 squares (this is a 3 digit by 2 digit sum). Draw in the diagonals and place the digits of each number across the top and down the side.

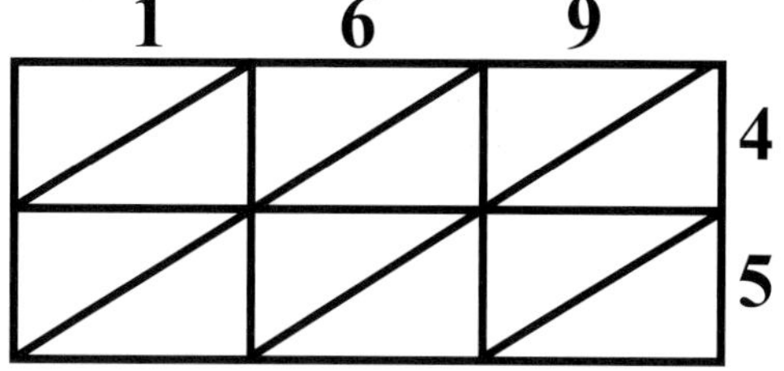


### Stage 2

Multiply each pair of digits and write the answer in the two spaces created by the diagonal. The tens digit (even if a zero) goes in the top left space and the units go in the bottom right space.

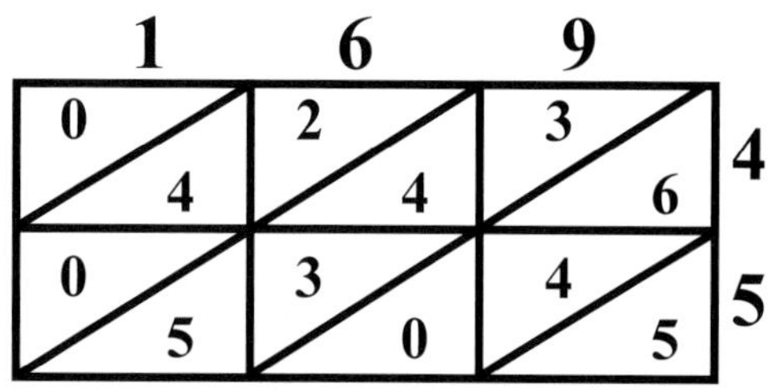


   

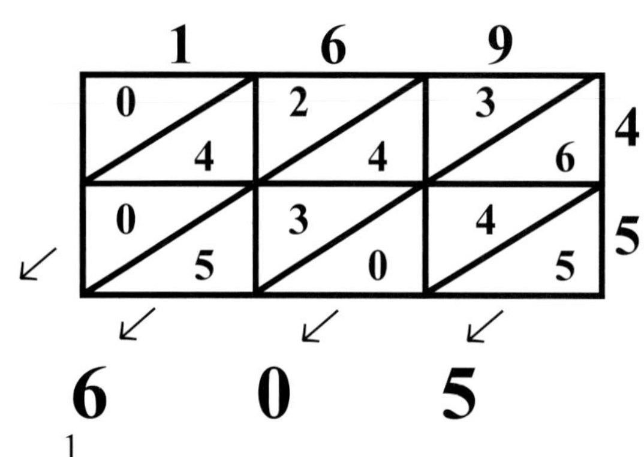

**Stage 3**

Add up the numbers along each diagonal 'path' starting at the bottom right hand corner. Don't forget to carry (it is necessary twice here). Reading the numbers from left to right gives the final answer.

**169 × 45 = 7,605**

---

# Exercise 2: 6  Calculate the following:   **Score**

1)  Multiply **579** and **33**.

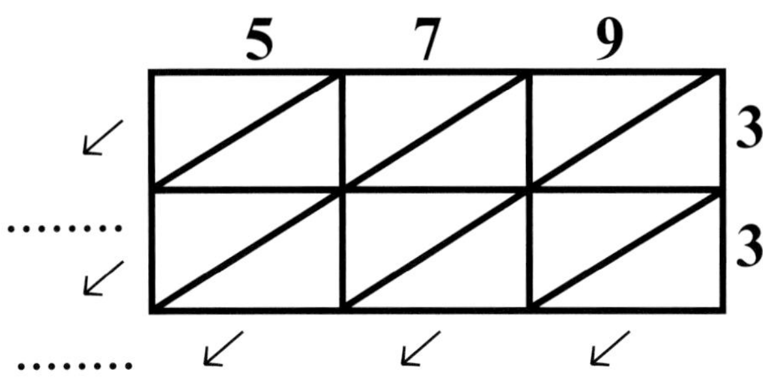

The answer is ................

2)  Multiply **49** by **17**.

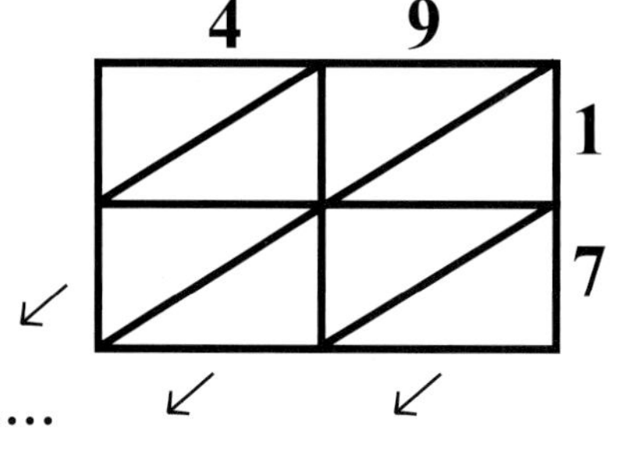

The answer is ...............

3)  Multiply **88** by **21**.

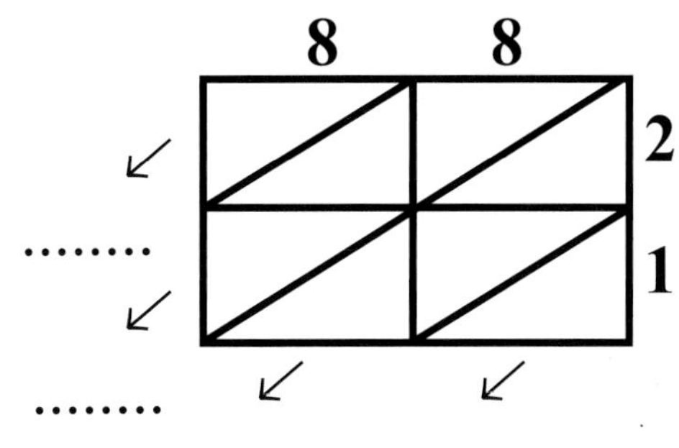

The answer is ................

4)  Multiply **325** and **67**.

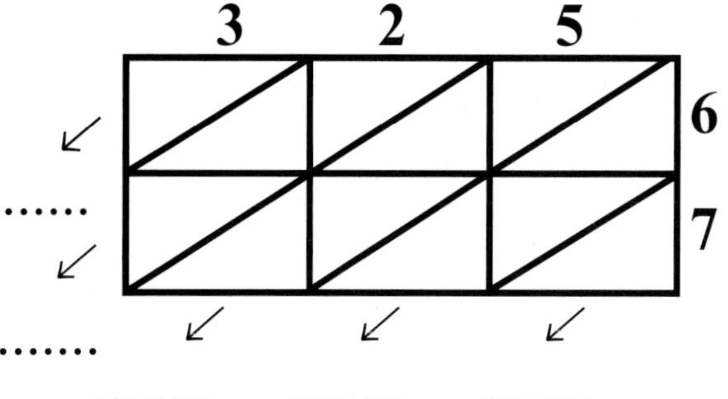

The answer is ...............

Using the 'Napier's Bones' method, do the following sums:

5)  **55 × 99**  =  .............

6)  **777 × 65**  =  .............

7)  **647 × 47**  =  .............

8)  **43 × 975**  =  .............

9)  **219 × 89**  =  .............

10)  **41 × 66**  =  .............

---

# 7. Box Method Multiplication

Box Method Multiplication is another way of Multiplying.

Example: **Multiply 155 by 19.**

### Step 1

Draw a box 3 squares by 2 squares (this is a 3 digit by 2 digit sum). Split the numbers into their hundreds, tens and units along the top and down the side.

$$155 = 100 + 50 + 5$$
$$19 = 10 + 9$$

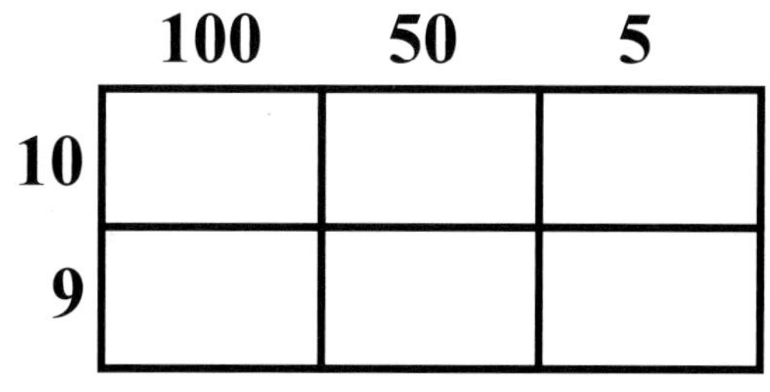

### Step 2

Multiply the numbers at the top and the numbers at the side and put the answer in each box.

|     | 100  | 50  | 5  |
|-----|------|-----|----|
| 10  | 1000 | 500 | 50 |
| 9   | 900  | 450 | 45 |

```
    1 0 0 0
      5 0 0
        5 0
      9 0 0
      4 5 0
        4 5 +
    ─────────
    2 9 4 5
```

### Step 3

Take the numbers from the box and write them down, lining up the units on the right. Then Add up the numbers.

## The answer is 2945

---

# Exercise 2: 7  Calculate the following:   Score

1) Multiply **342** and **21**.

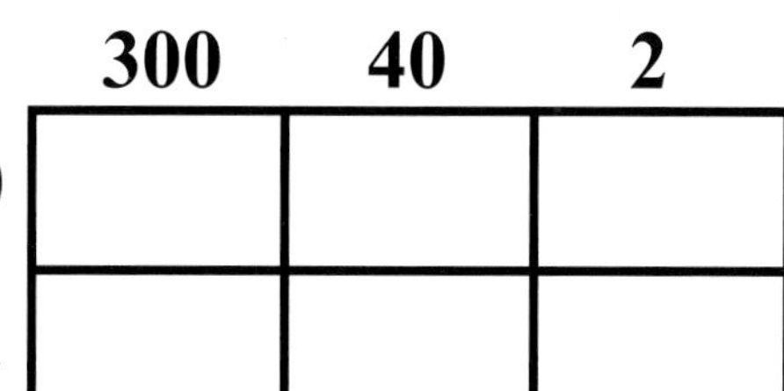

The answer is ...............

2) Multiply **39** by **15**.

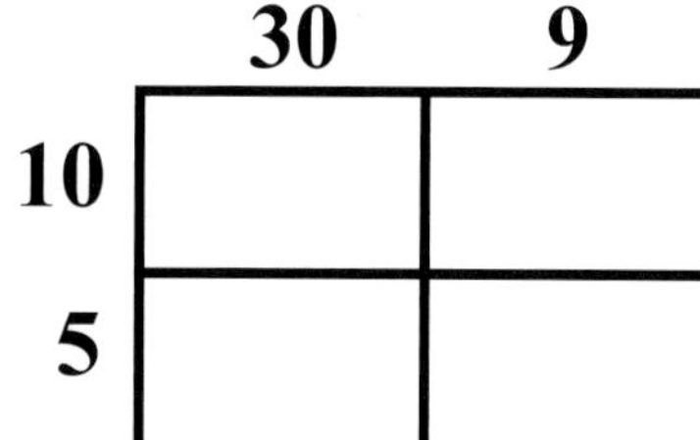

The answer is ...............

3) Multiply **78** by **38**.

|  | **70** | **8** |
|---|---|---|
| **30** |  |  |
| **8** |  |  |

The answer is ................

4) Multiply **524** and **53**.

|  | **500** | **20** | **4** |
|---|---|---|---|
| **50** |  |  |  |
| **3** |  |  |  |

The answer is ...............

Do the following sums using Box Method Multiplication:

5) **52 × 69** = .............

6) **666 × 77** = .............

7) **323 × 36** = .............

8) **23 × 765** = .............

9) **199 × 99** = .............

10) **47 × 68** = .............

# 8. *Multiply by Repeated Addition*

**Long Multiplication** can also be done by a process of **Repeated Addition**. The sum is split into tens, fives and units and Multiplied separately, then Added to find the Total.

Example: Multiply **47** by **179**.

1. **Multiply** by the tens.
(**10 × 179**)

2. **Multiply** by the fives.
(**5 × 179**)

3. **Multiply** by the ones.
(**1 × 179**)

4. **Add** the Amounts to find the Total.

$$10 \times 179 = 1790$$
$$10 \times 179 = 1790$$
$$10 \times 179 = 1790$$
$$10 \times 179 = 1790$$
$$5 \times 179 = 895$$
$$1 \times 179 = 179$$
$$1 \times 179 = 179 +$$

$$47 \times 179 = 8413$$

1) Multiply **139** by **43**.

$10 \times 139 = 1390$
$10 \times 139 = \dots\dots\dots$
$10 \times 139 = \dots\dots\dots$
$10 \times 139 = \dots\dots\dots$
$1 \times 139 = \dots\dots\dots$
$1 \times 139 = \dots\dots\dots$
$1 \times 139 = \dots\dots\dots +$

$43 \times 139 = \dots\dots\dots$

2) Multiply **77** by **35**.

$10 \times 77 = 770$
$10 \times 77 = \dots\dots$
$10 \times 77 = \dots\dots$
$5 \times 77 = \dots\dots +$

$35 \times 77 = \dots\dots$

Set out the last three sums on paper in the way shown and calculate:

3) Multiply **241** by **44**.
$= \dots\dots\dots$

4) Multiply **324** by **38**.
$= \dots\dots\dots$

5) Multiply **412** by **59**.
$= \dots\dots\dots$

# 9. Divide by Repeated Subtraction

**Long Division** can also be done by a process of **Repeated Subtraction**.

Example: Divide **1189** by **47**.

1. **Multiply: $10 \times 47$** is **470**, which is not as big as **1189** so **Subtract 470**.

2. **Repeat** the **Multiply** and **Take away 470** again.

3. **Multiply: $5 \times 47$** is **235**, which is smaller than **249** so **Minus 235**.

$$1189$$
$$10 \times 47 = 470 -$$
$$719$$
$$10 \times 47 = 470 -$$
$$249$$
$$+5 \times 47 = 235 -$$

Ans. **25**        rem. **1 4**

4. **Add** the number of times **47** has been multiplied (**25×**) and do the final Subtraction to find the Remainder (**14**).

6) Divide **557** by **29**.

$$10 \times 29 = 290 -$$
$$5 \times 29 = 145 -$$
$$+\,4 \times 29 = 116 -$$
Rem. ______

7) Divide **783** by **45**.

$$10 \times 45 = 450 -$$
$$5 \times 45 = 225 -$$
$$+\,2 \times 45 = 90 -$$
Rem. ______

**Score**

Set out these three sums on paper and calculate:

8) $783 \div 67$

= ..................

9) $1095 \div 55$

= ..................

10) $899 \div 38$

= ..................

# 10. Approximating Numbers

**Approximate** means 'near enough'. It is a rough guide.
Example: $\boxed{9 \times 98}$ when calculated comes to **882 exactly**.
For 'easy numbers' we make the **98** into **100**.
$9 \times 100$ would give an **Approximate Answer of 900**.

**Round Numbers** give a 'near enough' answer by taking the number up or down to the nearest Power of ten.

To the nearest 10      **432** would be → **430**

To the nearest 100      **167** would be → **200**

To the nearest 1,000      **3,400** would be → **3,000**

A Number of **5 or more Rounds Up**; **4 or less Rounds Down**. Example: **25** would round up to **30** (nearest ten).

**Exercise 2: 9** Round these numbers to the:

**Score**

| Nearest 10 | Nearest 100 | Nearest 1,000 |
|---|---|---|
| 1) **26** ......... | 3) **348** ......... | 5) **2,500** ......... |
| 2) **555** ......... | 4) **177** ......... | 6) **6,366** ......... |

Approximate these Sums ($\approx$ means 'nearly equal to'):

7) $21 + 68 \approx$ ..........    8) $5 \times 29 \approx$ ..........

9) $303 - 148 \approx$ ..........    10) $605 \div 21 \approx$ ..........

# 11. Odd and Even Numbers

**Even Numbers** -  2  4  6  8  10  12  14  16  18 etc.
(End with either  0, 2, 4, 6 or 8  e.g. 132, 400, 964, 78)

**Odd Numbers** -  1  3  5  7  9  11  13  15  17  19 etc.
(End with either  1, 3, 5, 7 or 9  e.g. 103, 81, 319, 495)

Even Numbers Divide by **2**. Odd Numbers don't Divide by **2**.

## Exercise 2: 10 Write Odd or Even by each number:

1) **27** ........    2) **82** ........    3) **999** ........    4) **866** ........

5) **497** ........    6) **77** ........    7) **800** ........    8) **54** ........

9) List the numbers from above that are **Divisible** by **2**.

........    ........    ........    ........    Score ☐

10) **1,989** does/does not Divide by **2** - underline.

# 12. Squares
## a. Square Numbers

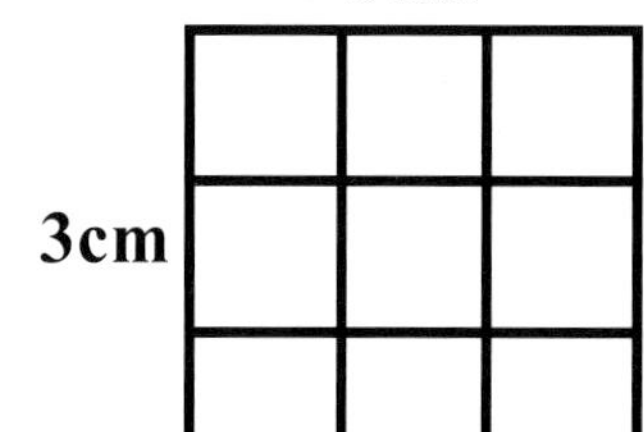


A **Square Number** is a number Multiplied by itself. It is based on the shape of a square.

$$3\text{cm} \times 3\text{cm} = 9\text{cm}^2$$

Example: What is $3^2$?   $3^2 = 3 \times 3 = 9$

(The small $^2$ means 'to the Power of 2'.)

## Exercise 2: 11 Write the Square of the following:

1) $4^2 =$ .......    2) $7^2 =$ .......    3) $9^2 =$ .......

4) $12^2 =$ ........    5) $6^2 =$ .......    6) $16^2 =$ .........

## b. Square Roots

A **Square Root** is the number a Square has come from.

Example: What is the Square Root of **9**?  $3^2 = 3 \times 3 = 9$

Hence **3** is the Square Root of **9**. It is the Inverse operation.

Square $\longleftrightarrow$ Square Root.   Square Root is written $\sqrt{\phantom{0}}$

so $\sqrt{9} = 3$ (The Square Root of **9** is **3**)

### Exercise 2: 12   Write the Square Roots of the following:

| 1) $\sqrt{4}$ = ......... | 2) $\sqrt{25}$ = ......... |
| 3) $\sqrt{100}$ = ......... | 4) $\sqrt{16}$ = ......... |
| 5) $\sqrt{36}$ = ......... | 6) $\sqrt{64}$ = ......... |
| 7) $\sqrt{49}$ = ......... | 8) $\sqrt{121}$ = ......... |
| 9) $\sqrt{81}$ = ......... | 10) $\sqrt{144}$ = ......... |

**Score**

# 13. Cubes
## a. Cube Numbers

A **Cube Number** is Multiplied by itself twice. It is based on the shape of a Cube.

Example: What is $3^3$?

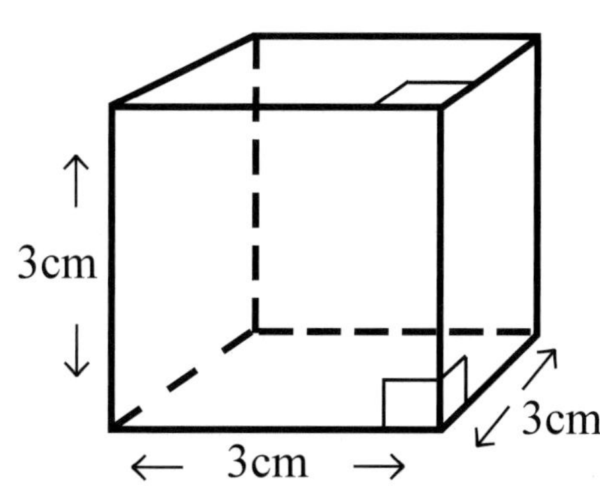


**3** Cubed $(3^3) = 3 \times 3 \times 3 = 27$

To Cube means to raise a number 'to the Power of 3'.

$$3^3 = 27$$

**Exercise 2: 13** Write the Cubes of the following:

1) $2^3$ = ..........        2) $4^3$ = ..........

3) $6^3$ = ..........        4) $7^3$ = ..........

5) $5^3$ = ..........        6) $9^3$ = ..........

7) $10^3$ = ..........        8) $8^3$ = ..........   Score

9) $12^3$ = ..........        10) $11^3$ = ..........

## b. Cube Roots

A **Cube Root** is the number a Cube has come from.

Example: | What is the Cube Root of **27**?

$3^3$ = **3** × **3** × **3** = **27** so **3** is the Cube Root of **27**.

Cube $\longleftrightarrow$ Cube Root    A Cube Root is written as $\sqrt[3]{\phantom{x}}$

so $\sqrt[3]{27}$ = **3** (The Cube Root of **27** is **3**).

**Exercise 2: 14** (Use the table on the next page for help.)  Score

Write Cube Roots for the following:

1) $\sqrt[3]{64}$ = ..........        2) $\sqrt[3]{125}$ = ..........

3) $\sqrt[3]{8}$ = ..........        4) $\sqrt[3]{512}$ = ..........

5) $\sqrt[3]{216}$ = ..........        6) $\sqrt[3]{1000}$ = ..........

7) $\sqrt[3]{27}$ = ..........        8) $\sqrt[3]{729}$ = ..........

9) $\sqrt[3]{343}$ = ..........        10) $\sqrt[3]{1331}$ = ..........

   

| Root | Square | Root | Square | | Root | Cube |
|------|--------|------|--------|---|------|------|
| 1 | 1 | 11 | 121 | | 1 | 1 |
| 2 | 4 | 12 | 144 | | 2 | 8 |
| 3 | 9 | 13 | 169 | | 3 | 27 |
| 4 | 16 | 14 | 196 | | 4 | 64 |
| 5 | 25 | 15 | 225 | | 5 | 125 |
| 6 | 36 | 16 | 256 | | 6 | 216 |
| 7 | 49 | 17 | 289 | | 7 | 343 |
| 8 | 64 | 18 | 324 | | 8 | 512 |
| 9 | 81 | 19 | 361 | | 9 | 729 |
| 10 | 100 | 20 | 400 | | 10 | 1000 |

# 14. Indices

The Power of a number is also called the **Index**.
If there are more than one they are termed **Indices**.

A number can be to any Power or Index.

Example: What is **2** to the **Power of 5** ($2^5$)?

$2^5$ (**2** to the Power of **five**) is **2** Multiplied by itself **4** times.

$$2^5 = 2 \times 2 \times 2 \times 2 \times 2 = 32$$

| | Once | Twice | 3 times | 4 times | |
|---|------|-------|---------|---------|---|
| | 4 | 8 | 16 | 32 | |

## Exercise 2: 15   Write the value of the following:

1) $2^4$ = ..........

2) $1^5$ = ..........

3) $3^4$ = ..........

4) $5^4$ = ..........

5) $3^6$ = ..........

6) $2^6$ = ..........

7) $3^5$ = ..........

8) $4^5$ = ..........

9) $5^5$ = ..........

10) $4^4$ = ..........

Score

# 15. Prime Numbers

A **Prime Number** has only two Factors (**itself** and **1**). It is a number which will not Divide by anything else but **itself** and **1**.

Example: | What are the Prime Numbers between 1 and 9?

$$1, \ \underline{\textbf{2}}, \ \underline{\textbf{3}}, \ 4, \ \underline{\textbf{5}}, \ 6, \ \underline{\textbf{7}}, \ 8, \ 9$$

**Factors** $(1, 2) (1, 3) (1, 5)$ $\qquad (1, 7)$

**2, 3, 5** and **7** are Prime Numbers.

Each number is only Divisible by **itself** and **1**.

---

- The first ten Prime Numbers are:

  **2, 3, 5, 7, 11, 13, 17, 19, 23** and **29**

- All Prime Numbers are Odd, except **2**.

- **1** is not a Prime Number (it has only one factor - itself).

- Prime Numbers do not appear in any other times tables.

- Prime Numbers usually end in **1, 3, 7** or **9**.

---

## Exercise 2: 16

Score

Write whether they are **Prime** or **Not Prime**:

1) **12** is ......................
2) **17** is ......................

3) **15** is ......................
4) **23** is ......................

5) **19** is ......................
6) **27** is ......................

7) **43** is ......................
8) **32** is ......................

9) **13** is ......................
10) **45** is ......................

   © 2006  Stephen Curran 

# 16. Rectangular Numbers

**Rectangular Numbers** are based on Rectangles (which includes Squares).

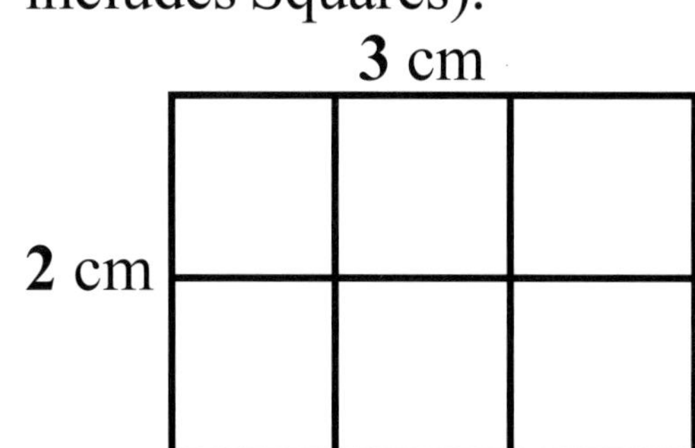

3 cm

2 cm

Example:

Is **6** a Rectangular Number?

**6** is a Rectangular Number because **3**cm $\times$ **2**cm = **6** cm$^2$

As a dot pattern $\rightarrow$ 

- All Even Numbers except **2** are Rectangular.
- Prime Numbers are never Rectangular.
- The first Six Rectangular Numbers - **4**, **6**, **8**, **9**, **10**, **12**

## Exercise 2: 17

**Score**

Are the following numbers Rectangular?

1) **15** yes/ no     2) **17** yes/ no

3) **25** yes/ no     4) **20** yes/ no

5) **50** yes/ no     6) **36** yes/ no

What Rectangular Numbers do the following make?

7) **6** and **4** = ........     8) **5** and **9** = ........

9) **9** and **8** = ........     10) **6** and **2** = ........

# 17. Triangular Numbers

**Triangular Numbers** are based on a Triangular pattern.

Example:    **1**      **3**      **6**      **10**

The first 4 Triangular Numbers:

Start with 1    Add 2    Add 3    Add 4

For the fifth Triangular Number add 5 and so on.

$$1 \; {}^{+2} \quad 3 \; {}^{+3} \quad 6 \; {}^{+4} \quad 10 \; {}^{+5} \quad 15 \; {}^{+6} \quad \text{etc.}$$

## Exercise 2: 18

Score

Write the following Triangular Numbers:

1) The **5th** is ..........

2) The **8th** is ..........

3) The **7th** is ..........

4) The **10th** is ..........

5) The **9th** is ..........

6) The **6th** is ..........

Add two Triangular Numbers to make the following:

7) **25** = ........ + ........

8) **16** = ........ + ........

9) **9** = ........ + ........

10) **31** = ........ + ........

# 18. Number Sequences

**Number Sequences** are series of numbers connected by rules, which create patterns.

| | |
|---|---|
| **Add or Subtract the Same Number.** <br> ${}^{+2} \quad {}^{+2} \quad {}^{+2} \quad {}^{+2} \quad {}^{+2}$ <br> **3, 5, 7, 9, 11, 13** | Example 1: <br> Add **2** to the previous number. <br> The next term will be **15** |
| **Add the Previous Two Terms.** <br> $2+4 \quad 4+6 \quad 6+10 \quad 10+16$ <br> **2, 4, 6, 10, 16, 26** | Example 2: <br> Add the two previous terms to get the next. <br> The next term will be **42** |
| **Add or Subtract a Changing Number.** <br> ${}^{-1} \quad {}^{-2} \quad {}^{-3} \quad {}^{-4}$ <br> **28, 27, 25, 22, 18** | Example 3: <br> Subtract **1**, then **2**, then **3** etc. <br> The next term will be **13** |



© 2006 Stephen Curran 

**Multiply or Divide by the Same Number.**

$$3, \overset{\times 2}{\phantom{x}} 6, \overset{\times 2}{\phantom{x}} 12, \overset{\times 2}{\phantom{x}} 24, \overset{\times 2}{\phantom{x}} 48$$

Example 4:

| Multiply the previous number by **2**. |

The next will be **96**

**Multiply or Divide by a Changing Number.**

$$6{,}000, \overset{\div 5}{\phantom{x}} 1{,}200, \overset{\div 4}{\phantom{x}} 300, \overset{\div 5}{\phantom{x}} 60$$

Example 5:

| Divide by **5**, then by **4**, then by **5** etc. |

The next will be **15**

- - -

Number Sequences come in many forms - watch out for:
- Combined operations. e.g. Multiply by **3**, then Add **2** etc.
- Square and Cube numbers. e.g. **4**, **9**, **16**, **25**, **36** etc.

## Exercise 2: 19a   Write in the Missing Numbers:

1) **55, 46, 37, 28,** ....., .....

2) **2, 6, 18,** ....., .....

3) **5, 11, 17, 23,** ....., .....

4) **0, 2, 6,** ....., **20,** .....

5) **8, 27, 64,** ....., .....

6) **3, 4, 2, 5, 1,** ....., .....

Number Sequences can be made using diagrams.

Example: | What Sequence does this pattern make? |

Count the sides. The gap between them increases by **3** each time.

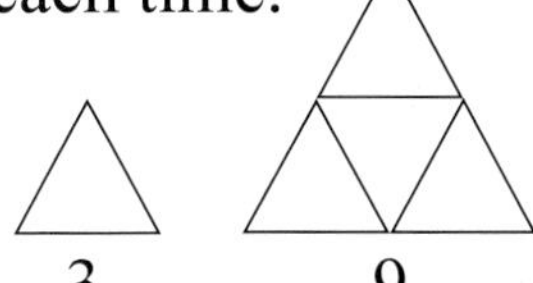


The pattern is   $3, \overset{+6}{\phantom{x}} 9, \overset{+9}{\phantom{x}} 18$

The next three numbers:

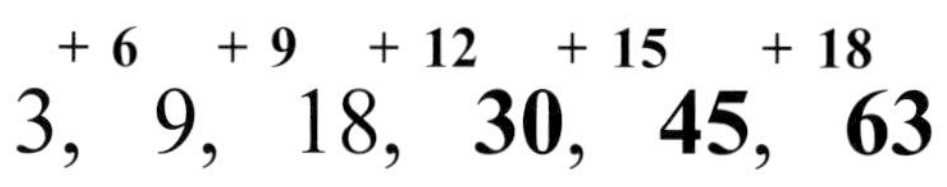

$$3, \overset{+6}{\phantom{x}} 9, \overset{+9}{\phantom{x}} 18, \overset{+12}{\phantom{x}} \mathbf{30}, \overset{+15}{\phantom{x}} \mathbf{45}, \overset{+18}{\phantom{x}} \mathbf{63}$$

## Exercise 2: 19b   Write the next two numbers:

**Score**

7) 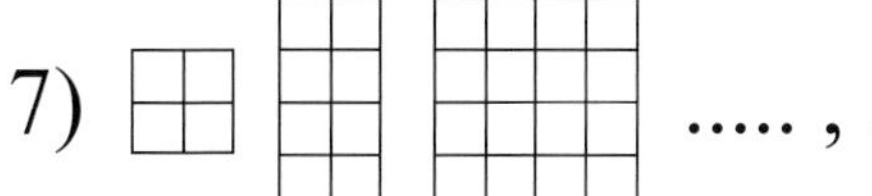 ....., .....

8) 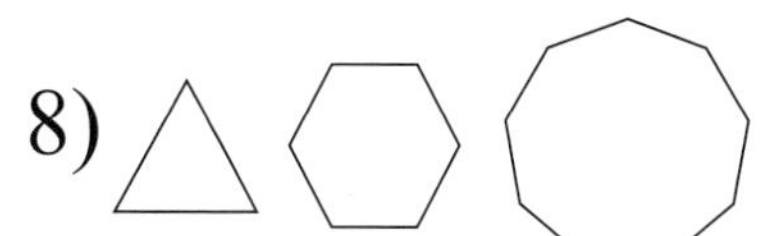 ....., .....

9)  ....., .....   10) ....., .....

# 19. Number Lines

Numbers are sometimes shown on a Number Line. Missing Numbers are found by examining the given sequence.

Example: What are the missing Numbers on this Number Line?

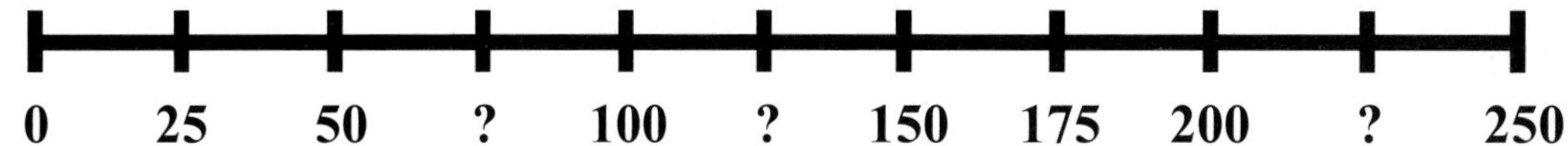


The Sequence rises by **25** each time. The missing Numbers are **75**, **125** and **225**.

---

## Exercise 2: 20 What are the Missing Numbers:

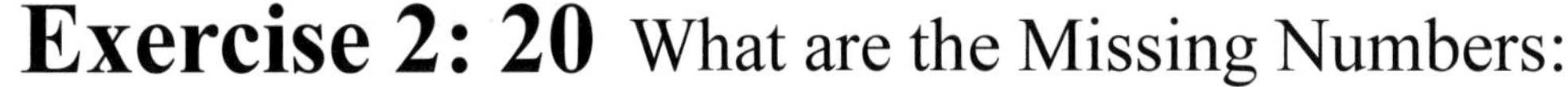


1-2) The Missing Numbers are .......... ..........

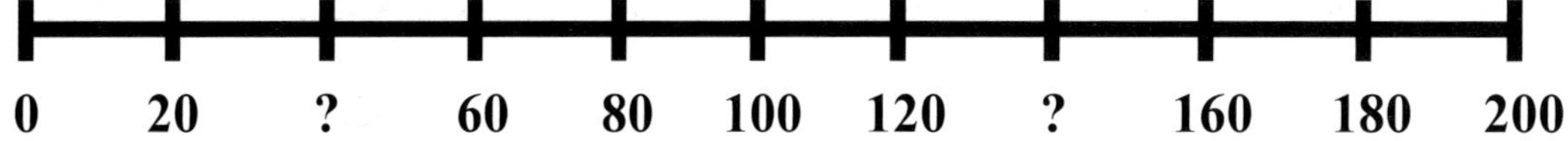


3-4) The Missing Numbers are .......... ..........

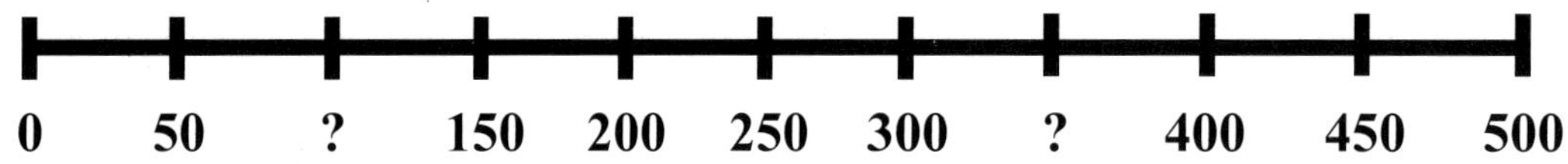


5-7) The Missing Numbers are .......... .......... ..........

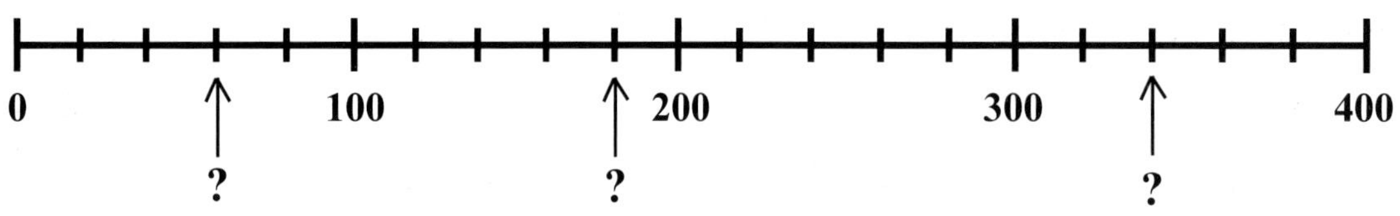


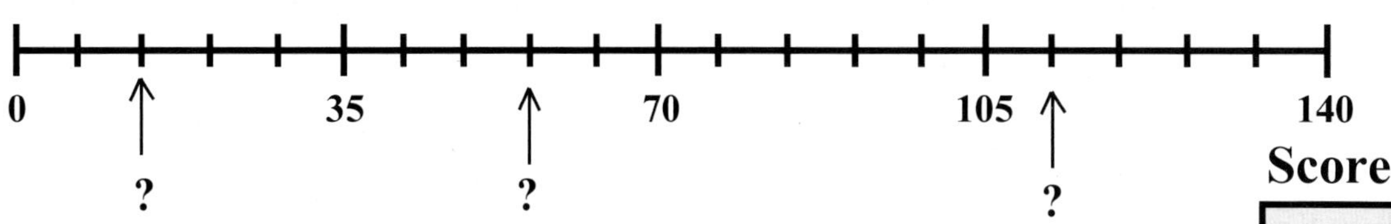

**Score**

8-10) The Missing Numbers are .......... .......... ..........

 

# 20. Positive & Negative Numbers

Whole Numbers (**Integers**) can be Positive or Negative.
**Positive** and **Negative Numbers** are also known as **Directed Numbers** and can be represented on a **Number Line** (known as an **Integer Line** if it shows Whole numbers only).

**Positive** (+ Plus numbers)        1,  17,  63

**Negative** ( − Minus numbers)   -5, -10, -23

*The signs (+ & -) show the **direction** of the numbers.*

Use the **Integer Line** - Count the gaps, not the Digits.
Remember:  If counting in your head, include the zero as you count up or down.

Example:
> What is the gap between **-2** and **3**?

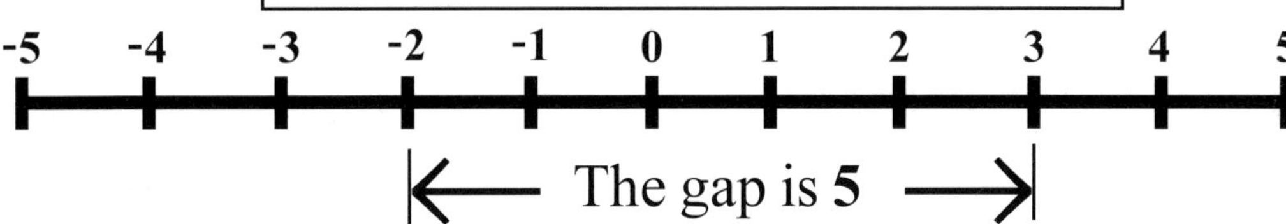

The gap is **5**

**Temperature questions** often use Negative and Positive values.

## Exercise 2: 21a    Use the Integer Line to count:

Write the gap between  1)  **-5** and **4** ?  .....  2) **2** and **-1** ? .....

3)  On a winter evening the Temperature was **7$^{o}$C**.  It fell by **8$^{o}$C**. What is the new Temperature? .........

4)  The Temperature in Scotland fell by **5$^{o}$C** overnight. It started out as **zero$^{o}$C**. What was the new Temperature by morning? ........

5)  What is the difference in Temperature between?  **-3$^{o}$C** and **7$^{o}$C** ?  .........

Numbers to the right are Bigger and to the left are Smaller.

⟵ (Smaller than) <   > (Bigger than) ⟶

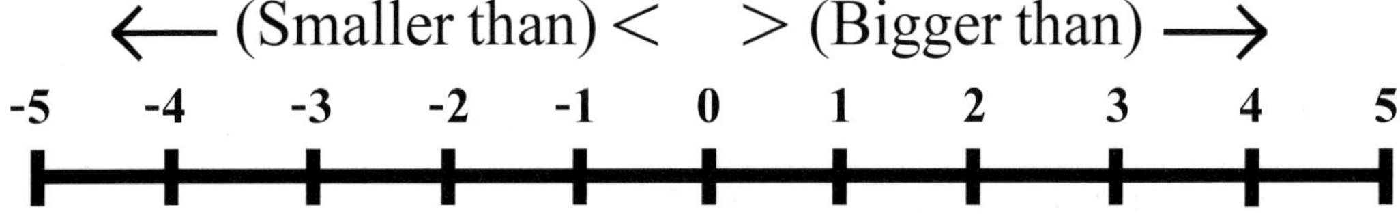

The signs $<$ (Smaller than) and $>$ (Bigger than) show the relationship between two numbers.

**An Easy Rule**: 'The mouth of the crocodile (open end) always swallows the biggest number'.

Examples: | Use < or > between these Numbers. |

$$1 > -2 \qquad -5 < 5 \qquad -1 > -4 \qquad -3 < 0$$

## Exercise 2: 21b   Answer the following:

6)   Put the signs > or < between these pairs of numbers:

   a)  **-3      2**    b)  **-8      10**    c)  **2      -7**

7)   Put these numbers in order  **-10, 5, -5, -2, 8, -1, 10** lowest first:   ......   ......   ......   ......   ......   ......   ......

**Adding and Subtracting Directed Numbers**. 2 rules:-
• Always start Counting at zero.
• Count <u>right</u> for Positive/<u>left</u> for Negative Numbers.

Example: | Work out  **+2  -3  -1** |    **+2  -3  -1  =  -2**

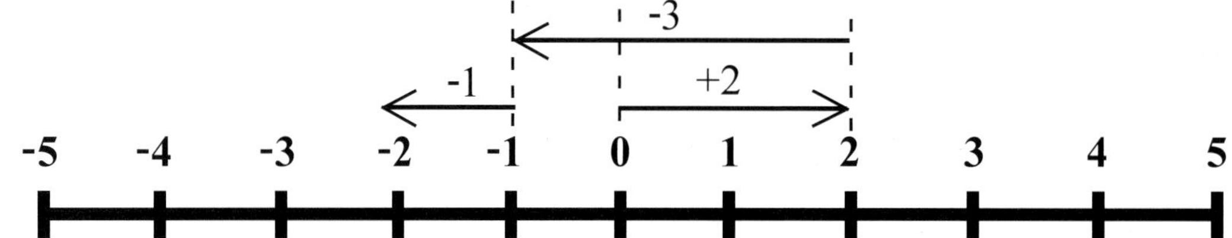


## Exercise 2: 21c   Calculate the following:   **Score**

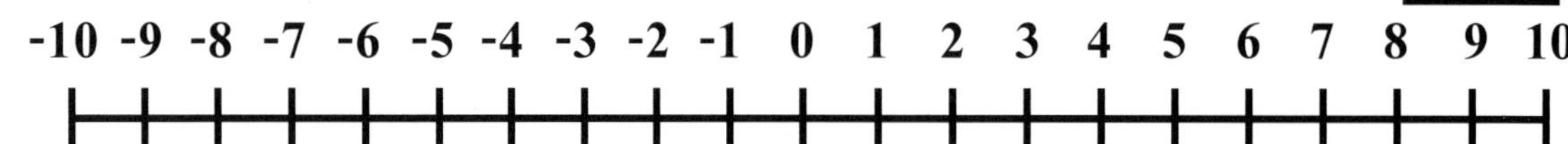


8)  **-6  -4  +14  =**  ............    9)  **-1  -7  +9  =**  ............

10)  **+10  -7  +3  -13  =**  ............

   

# 21. Factors
## a. What is a Factor?

**Factors** are numbers that Divide into one or more numbers exactly without Remainders.

Example: What are the Factors of **24**?

**These numbers all Divide into 24.**

**1, 2, 3, 4, 6, 8, 12** and **24** are all Factors of **24**.

---

**Exercise 2: 22** Find the Factors of the following numbers:  Score

1)  **45** .................................
2)  **20** .................................

3)  **15** .................................
4)  **13** .................................

5)  **18** .................................
6)  **26** .................................

7)  **25** .................................
8)  **30** .................................

9)  **50** .................................
10) **48** .................................

## b. Common Factors

Numbers often share Factors common to each other.

Example: Give the Common Factors of **12** and **18**:

**12**  **1**, **2**, **3**, 4, **6**, 12

**18**  **1**, **2**, **3**, **6**, 9, 18

The Common Factors of **12** and **18** are **1**, **2**, **3** and **6**.

---

**Exercise 2: 23a** <u>Underline</u> the Common Factors of:

1)  **6** and **12** (2, 3, 4, 6, 12)
2)  **16** and **24** (1, 2, 3, 4, 6, 8)

3)  **36** and **42** (3, 6, 7, 12)
4)  **15** and **30** (2, 3, 5, 10, 15)

# c. Highest Common Factors (HCF)

A **Highest Common Factor** (HCF) is the highest number that divides exactly into two (or more) other numbers.

Example: What is the HCF of **9, 27** and **36**?

| | | |
|---|---|---|
| **9** - 1, 3, **9** | | The **Highest** |
| **27** - 1, 3, **9**, 27 | | **Common Factor** |
| **36** - 1, 2, 3, 4, 6, **9**, 12, 18, 36 | | (**HCF**) is **9**. |

**Exercise 2: 23b** Find the HCF of the following:

Score

5)  **16, 25** and **36** ............  6)  **14** and **21** ............

7)  **12, 20** and **32** ............  8)  **56** and **72** ............

9)  **28, 36** and **56** ............  10)  **24** and **36** ............

# d. Prime Factors

A **Prime Factor** is a Prime Number that Divides into another number exactly.

Example: Express **2** and **3** as Prime Factors of **24**.

**2** and **3** are both Prime Factors of **24** because they are Prime Numbers and Divide into **24**.

**24** is expressed as a **Product** of its Prime Factors by using Indices.

$$2 \times 2 \times 2 \times 3$$
$$2^3 \times 3 = 24$$

**Exercise 2: 24** Write the Prime Factors of the following:

1)  **10** = ..............  2)  **15** = ..............

3)  **20** = ..............  4)  **14** = ..............

5)  **26** = ..............  6)  **12** = ..............

Write the missing Prime Factor:

**Score**

7) $2^2 \times$ ........ $= 12$   8) $3^2 \times$ ........ $= 18$

9) $2^3 \times$ ........ $= 40$   10) $5^2 \times$ ........ $= 50$

# 22. Multiples
## a. What is a Multiple?

A **Multiple** is any number in the times tables of a number.

Example: Multiples of **5** would be: **5, 10, 15, 20, 25**, etc.

## Exercise 2: 25  Write the next five Multiples: **Score**

1) **7** ..... ..... ..... ..... .....     2) **8** ..... ..... ..... ..... .....

3) **15** ..... ..... ..... ..... .....     4) **9** ..... ..... ..... ..... .....

5) **16** ..... ..... ..... ..... .....     6) **14** ..... ..... ..... ..... .....

7) **12** ..... ..... ..... ..... .....     8) **6** ..... ..... ..... ..... .....

9) **13** ..... ..... ..... ..... .....     10) **11** ..... ..... ..... ..... .....

## b. Common Multiples

Numbers often share Multiples common to each other.

Example: Give two Common Multiples of **4** and **6**:

**4** | 4, 8, **12**, 16, 20, **24**

**6** | 6, **12**, 18, **24**

**12** and **24** are Common Multiples as both numbers Divide by **4** and **6**.

## Exercise 2: 26a  <u>Underline</u> the Common Multiples of:

1) **3** and **4** (12, 15, 18, 21, 24)     2) **4** and **6** (36, 42, 48, 54)

3) **3** and **6** (9, 12, 15, 18)     4) **6** and **8** (12, 16, 24, 32, 48)

# c. Lowest Common Multiples (LCM)

The **Lowest (Least) Common Multiple** of two (or more) numbers is the smallest possible number into which all of them will Divide.

Example: | Give the **LCM** of **3**, **4** and **8**:

The lowest number that all three of these numbers will Divide into is **24**.

**3** 3, 6, 9, 12, 15, 18, 21, **24**

**4** 4, 8, 12, 16, 20, **24**

**8** 8, 16, **24**

**Written questions** also use **LCM**:  Example:

What is the smallest number of roses that can be arranged in bunches of either **3, 6** or **9**? | **Answer** is **18 Roses**.

## Exercise 2: 26b  What is the LCM of:   Score

5) **6** and **8** ......   6) **9** and **12** ......   7) **8, 9** and **12** ......

8) **6** and **7** ......   9) **7, 8** and **14** ......   10) **11** and **12** ......

# 23. Applied Number Problems

**Number Problems** require the use of:   $+ \ - \ \times \ \div$

Example:   (Four Rules of Number.)

A forest has **17** oak trees, twice as many beech trees and five times as many ash trees. How many trees are there?

$2 \times 17 =$     $5 \times 17 =$

**17 oak trees**  +  **34 trees**  +  **85 trees**  =  **136 trees**

## Exercise 2: 27   Calculate the following:

1)  An aeroplane has **150** seats. It leaves for New York from London with **35** Americans and **62** Britons. How many spare seats are there?  ............ (Add and Subtract.)

2) There are **250** children at Atwood School. **153** children have school meals and the others have packed lunches. How many do not have school meals? ............ (Subtract.)

3) Suitcases are being loaded into **5** coaches. Each coach can only hold **32** suitcases. There are **163** suitcases. Will there be enough room? Yes or no? ............ (Multiply.)

4) A shelf holds **42** books. How many shelves will be needed to house **294** books? ............ (Divide.)

5) In a cinema there are **13** rows of **22** seats on one side and **14** rows of **20** seats on the other side. How many seats in the cinema are there altogether? ............ (Multiply and Add.)

6) A bus without passengers leaves the depot. At the first stop **5** passengers get on. At the second stop **15** get on and **3** get off. At the third stop **8** get on and **5** get off. How many passengers are now on the bus?
............ (Add and Subtract.)

7) A caretaker looks after **23** classrooms in a school. He employs **3** cleaners who clean **7** classrooms each. How many classrooms does he clean himself? ............ (Multiply and Subtract.)

8) In 1996, **65** children passed their cycle proficiency test.
In 1997, **twice** as many passed as in 1996.
In 1998, **three times** as many passed as in 1997.
How many children passed in 1998? ............ (Multiply.)

9) School text books are being ordered. Each class needs **30** books. There are **7** classes in the school. How many books will need to be ordered? ............ (Multiply.)

10) On school sports day all the children are Divided into **6** teams. There are **330** children. How many children will there be in each team? ............ (Divide.)

**Score**

# 24. Roman Numerals

**Roman Numerals** are a useful alternative counting system.

Example 1: What symbols are used in Roman Numerals?

**I** = 1 : **V** = 5 : **X** = 10 : **L** = 50
**C** = 100 : **D** = 500 : **M** = 1,000

Example 2: Show the sequence of numbers from **1** to **10**.

| **I** | **II** | **III** | **IV** | **V** | **VI** | **VII** | **VIII** | **IX** | **X** |
|---|---|---|---|---|---|---|---|---|---|
| 1 | 2 | 3 | 4 | 5 | 6 | 7 | 8 | 9 | 10 |

Example 3: Write **4** and **9** using the **Subtraction Rule**.

**4** and **9** are made by Subtracting from 5 and 10.
The smaller Digit is Subtracted from the larger Digit.

**IV**    **IX**    **XIV**    **XL**

$5 - 1 = 4$    $10 - 1 = 9$    $10 + 5 - 1 = 14$    $50 - 10 = 40$

Example 4: Show how **1,500**, **1,750** and **2,664** are written.

**M D** — 1,500

**MD CC L** — 1,750

**MM DC LX IV** — 2,664

---

## Exercise 2: 28    Convert to Denary:    Score

1) **XXIV** .........    2) **CCXC** .........    3) **CDIX** .........

4) **DXXVI** .........    5) **MIX** .........    6) **DCCXL** .........

7) **MCCCXXI** .............    8) **MDCCCLIV** ...............

9) **MMCLV** ...............    10) **CMLVIII** ...............

# 25. Number Relationship Problems

**Exercise 2: 30**   Answer the following:   Score

1a)
A = ........
B = ........

| 13 | 20 | 15 |
| 18 | B |  |
| A |  | 14 |

b)
A = ........
B = ........

| 39 | 24 | 27 |
| B |  | A |
|  |  | 21 |

2a) $14^2$ = ..........   b) $2^7$ = ..........   c) $6^4$ = ..........

d) What is the Square Root of **169**? ..........

3a) Write the first five Rectangular Numbers?

........   ........   ........   ........   ........

b) Which of these numbers are Triangular? ...... ......

c) Add the Prime Numbers between **4** and **12**. ............

d) What Rectangular Number does this Dot Pattern represent? ........ 

------------------------------------------------

4) Write the next two numbers in the series:

a) **1, 4, 9, 16,** ...... , ......    b) **15, 30,** ...... , **63,** ......

------------------------------------------------

5a) What is the gap between **-3** and **4**? ..........

Work out b) **+4  -5  -2** .......... c) **-3  +4  -1** ..........

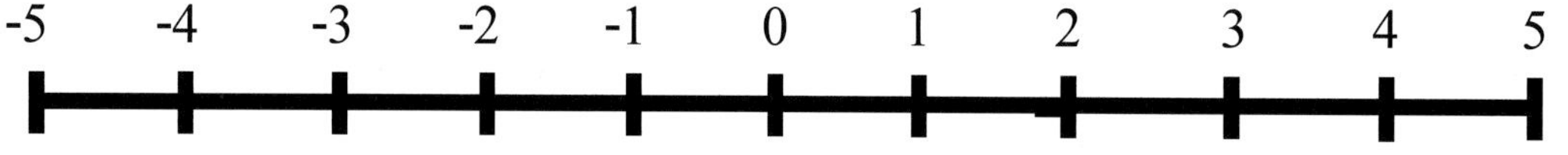

------------------------------------------------

6a) Write all the Factors of **64** ......................................

b) What is the Highest Common Factor (HCF) of: **36, 54** and **72**? ............

c) What are the Prime Factors of **30**? ....................

d) $3^2$ is a Prime Factor of **63**. What is the other Prime Factor? ............

------------------------------------------------

7) What is the Lowest Common Multiple (LCM) of:

a) **3, 5** and **4** ........    b) **7, 8** and **12** ........

c) **5, 7** and **10** ........

------------------------------------------------

8) A crate holds **10** bottles. Crates are packed in containers of **6**. How many bottles are packed in **8** containers? ............

------------------------------------------------

9) How many glasses of cola can be filled from **126** one litre bottles if each bottle holds **6** glasses? ............

------------------------------------------------

10) How many seats are there in a cinema that has **25** rows of **17** seats each side of the centre aisle? ............

# Chapter Three
# DECIMALS
## 1. Tens Number System

The **Tens Number System** can be extended into tenths, hundredths, thousandths etc.

Numbers can be placed on a **Decimal Table** (shown below) so that **Place Value** can be determined.

Whole number ⟵ | ⟶ Less than a whole one

| TH | H | T | U | t | h | th |
|----|----|----|----|----|----|----|
| 4 | 6 | 7 | 1 | 5 | 9 | 3 |

The **Decimal Point** separates the whole numbers from the Decimal Fractions.

**Key**

TH - Thousands
H - Hundreds
T - Tens
U - Units
t - tenths
h - hundredths
th - thousandths

This number has been written to three **Decimal Places**.

4 6 7 1 . 5 9 3

3 thousandths
9 hundredths
5 tenths
Whole number

Study the table to see how units, tenths, hundredths and thousandths are written.

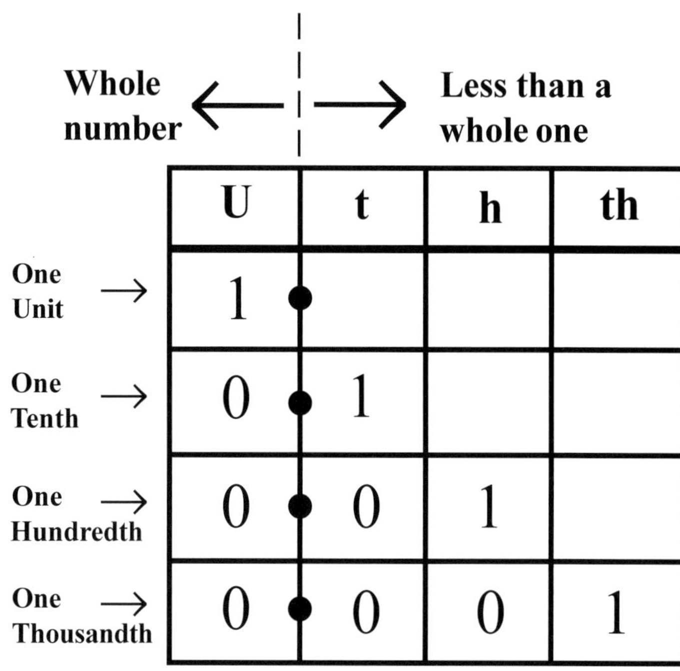



| | U | t | h | th |
|---|---|---|---|---|
| One Unit → | 1 | | | |
| One Tenth → | 0 | 1 | | |
| One Hundredth → | 0 | 0 | 1 | |
| One Thousandth → | 0 | 0 | 0 | 1 |

$$\rightarrow \quad 1 \div 10 = \frac{1}{10}$$

$$\rightarrow \quad \frac{1}{10} \div 10 = \frac{1}{100}$$

$$\rightarrow \quad \frac{1}{100} \div 10 = \frac{1}{1000}$$

This diagram compares the size of a unit, a tenth and a hundredth.

One Unit

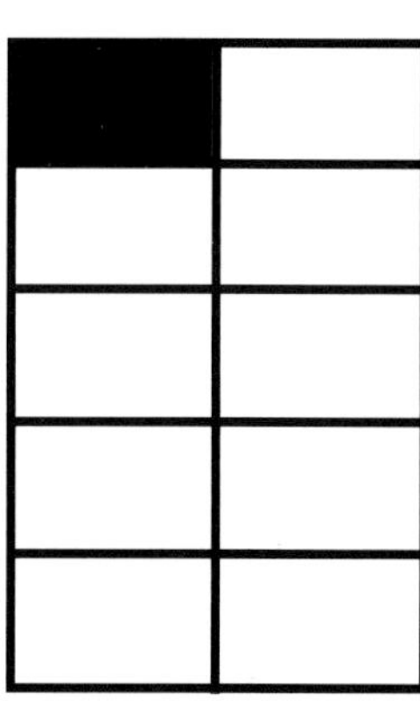

One Tenth

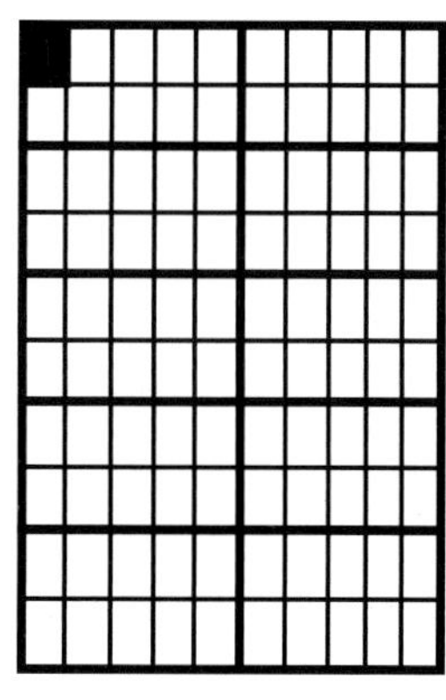

One Hundredth

It is written as: **1.1 1**

It could be expressed as:  1 unit, 1 tenth and 1 hundredth
**or**  11 tenths and 1 hundredth
**or**  1 unit and 11 hundredths
**or**  111 hundredths

# 2. Place Value
## a. Whole numbers as Decimals

All **Whole Numbers** can be expressed as a Decimal.

Example: Express **1** and **25** as Decimals.

Put a Decimal point after the number, followed by a zero.

1 can be written as **1.0**

25 can be written as **25.0**

### Exercise 3: 1    Express these Whole Numbers:

With a Decimal Point.

1) **6** ................
2) **71** ................
3) **59** ................
4) **566** ................
5) **4,988** ................

Without a Decimal Point.

6) **9.0** ................
7) **98.0** ................
8) **12.0** ................
9) **812.0** ................
10) **5,234.0** ................

**Score**

## b. The Decimal Table

Decimals can be placed on the Decimal Table for clarity.

Example: Place **3,256.324** on the Decimal Table.

Use the Decimal Point to correctly place the number.

| TH | H | T | U | t | h | th |
|----|----|----|----|----|----|----|
| 3 | 2 | 5 | 6 | 3 | 2 | 4 |

### Exercise 3: 2    Put these numbers on the Decimal Table:

**Score**

1) **34.12**
2) **0.129**

| TH | H | T | U | t | h | th |
|----|----|----|----|----|----|----|
| ...... | ...... | ...... | ...... | ...... | ...... | ...... |
| ...... | ...... | ...... | ...... | ...... | ...... | ...... |

3) **667.2**
4) **10.346**
5) **1,975.021**

Draw a Decimal Table and place these numbers on it.

6) **1.8**    7) **8.65**    8) **0.991**    9) **777.44**    10) **1,087.051**

## c. Value of Decimals

The **Value** of a Decimal Digit is indicated by its position in the number.

Example:

What is the value of the **2** in the number **5.624**?

$$5.624$$

Whole number — **6 tenths**, **2 hundredths**, **4 thousandths**

It would be **2 hundredths**.

**Exercise 3: 3** Write the **Value** of the following:    **Score**

1) The **6** in **2.612**    = ............................................

2) The **3** in **3.74**    = ............................................

3) The **9** in **0.941**    = ............................................

4) The **2** in **4.62**    = ............................................

5) The **3** in **55.453**    = ............................................

6) The **7** in **1.567**    = ............................................

**Underline** the required **Value** in the following:

7) **Thousandths** in  **0.012**         8) **Units** in  **1.67**

9) **Hundredths** in  **4.21**         10) **Tenths** in  **0.322**

# d. Expressing Decimal Values

The **Value** of a Decimal can be **expressed** as follows:

Example: Show **1.593** on the Decimal Table.

Whole number ⟵⎮⟶ Less than a whole one

| U | t | h | th |
|---|---|---|----|
| 1 • | 5 | 9 | 3 |

It can be expressed as: 1 unit, 5 tenths, nine hundredths, 3 thousandths.

**Note** that these are only a few examples of the ways the number can be expressed.

or   1 unit, 5 tenths, 93 thousandths.

or   1 unit, 593 thousandths.

or   1593 thousandths.

## Exercise 3: 4    Write the Value of the following:

1) **0.661** in thousandths = ...........................................

2) **1.12** in hundredths = ...........................................

3) **41.32** in tens, units, tenths and hundredths = .........
...........................................................................

4) **5.78** in units and hundredths = ...........................
...........................................................................

5) **66.728** in units and thousandths = .......................
...........................................................................

6) **0.015** in thousandths = .......................................

7) **79.01** in hundredths = .........................................

8) **8.72** in units and hundredths = ...............................

..................................................................................

9) **105.8** in tenths = ....................................... **Score**

10) **6.9** in tenths = .......................................

# e. Decimals in Value Order

It is important to be able to put Decimals in **order of size**.

Example: | Arrange the Decimals in size order, smallest first.
0.8          0.019          0.97

- Draw the Decimal Table and put the numbers on it.
- Make the numbers into a box by filling up the spaces with zeros.
- All the numbers are now thousandths.

| U | t | h | th |
|---|---|---|---|
| 0 | 8 | 0 | 0 | → 800 thousandths
| 0 | 0 | 1 | 9 | → 19 thousandths
| 0 | 9 | 7 | 0 | → 970 thousandths

The order, smallest first, is as follows:
**0.019          0.8          0.97**

## Exercise 3: 5                                        **Score**

Write the following Decimals in **size order, smallest first**.

1) **1.6    1.09    1.306**          2) **0.001    0.1    0.01**

......... ......... .........          ......... ......... .........

3) **3.8    1.21    0.55**          4) **1.9    0.99    0.1**

......... ......... .........          ......... ......... .........

          

| 5) | **1.33** | **1.213** | **1.4** | | 6) | **3.71** | **2.9** | **3.8** |
| --- | --- | --- | --- | --- | --- | --- | --- | --- |
| ......... | ......... | ......... | | | ......... | ......... | ......... |

Write the following in **size order**, **largest first**.

| 7) | **2.13** | **2.9** | **3** | | 8) | **1.012** | **1.2** | **1.102** |
| --- | --- | --- | --- | --- | --- | --- | --- | --- |
| ......... | ......... | ......... | | | ......... | ......... | ......... |
| 9) | **14.1** | **1.141** | **0.41** | | 10) | **0.723** | **0.91** | **0.81** |
| ......... | ......... | ......... | | | ......... | ......... | ......... |

The size of Decimals can be shown in relation to each other by using the following signs.

$<$     $>$

(Smaller than)    (Bigger than)

Remember: The mouth of the crocodile always swallows the largest amount.

Example:

Smaller than

$$0.6 \; < \; 1.5$$

Bigger than

$$1.5 \; > \; 0.6$$

## Exercise 3: 6

Place 'Bigger than' or 'Smaller than' signs between these numbers:

| 1) | **0.04** | **3.2** | 2) | **0.167** | **0.2** |
| --- | --- | --- | --- | --- | --- |
| 3) | **1.07** | **0.157** | 4) | **54.158** | **54.185** |
| 5) | **1.058** | **1.06** | 6) | **2.018** | **2.009** |
| 7) | **0.6** | **0.47** | 8) | **0.03** | **0.027** |
| 9) | **5.19** | **3.599** | 10) | **0.076** | **0.11** |

Score

# *f. Number Lines and Decimals*

Decimal Number Sequences can appear confusing unless the smallest counting unit is clearly established.

Example: | What Number does the arrow point to?

The larger gap between **4.2** and **4.3** is a **tenth** of a unit (4.2 has 1 d.p.), so the smaller gaps are in **hundredths** of a unit.

1. Add zeros to **4.2 (4.20)** and **4.3 (4.30)** to change them to **hundredths** of a unit.

2. Treat **4.20** and **4.30** as Whole Numbers i.e. **420** and **430**. Label each missing gap, which is **2 hundredths** of a unit.

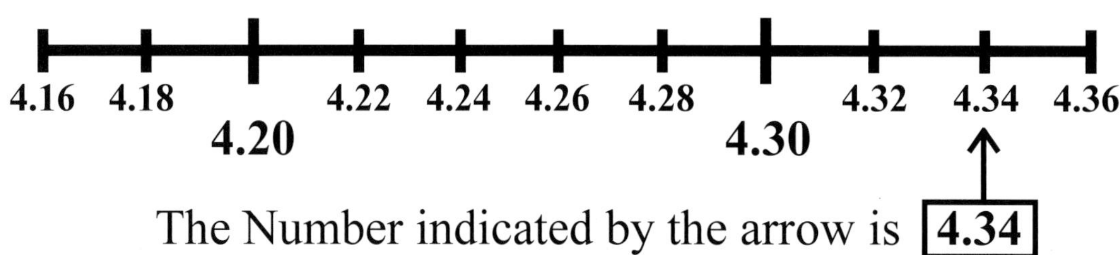


The Number indicated by the arrow is $\boxed{4.34}$

---

# Exercise 3: 7

Write the Numbers indicated:

Score

**Change to hundredths.**

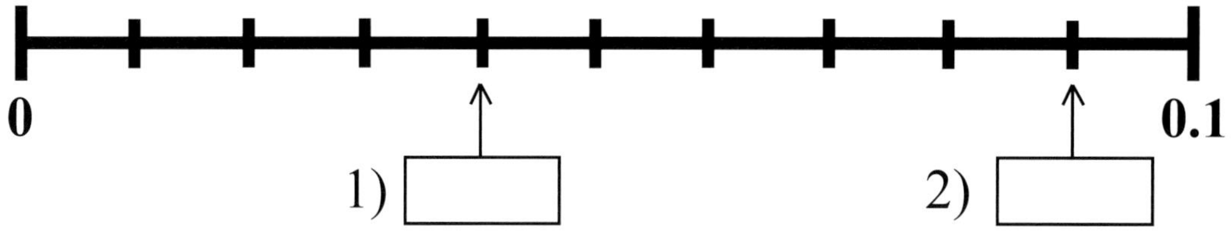

0

1)

2)

0.1

---

**Change to hundredths.**

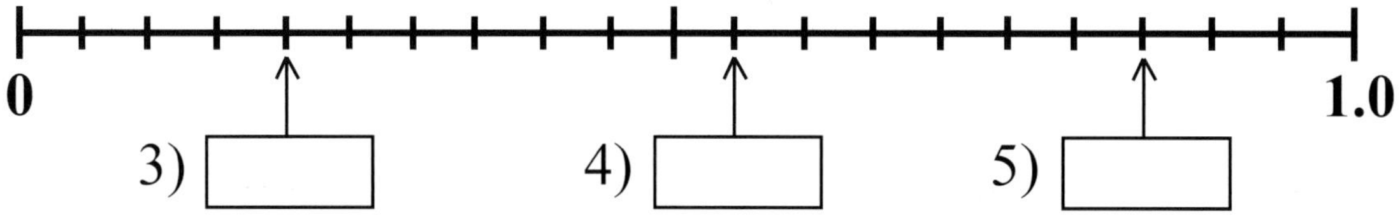

0

3)

4)

5)

1.0

---

**Change to thousandths.**

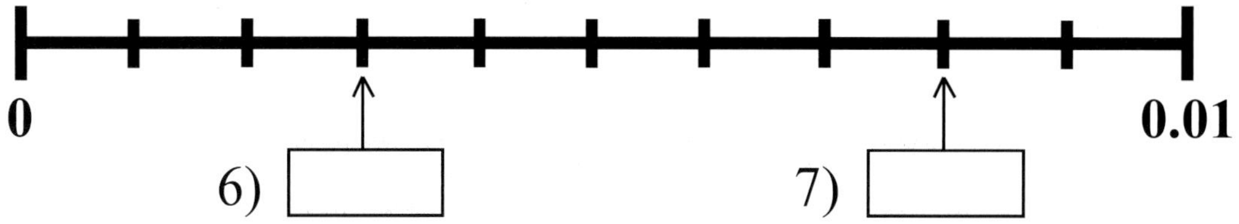

0

6)

7)

0.01

---

**Change to thousandths.**

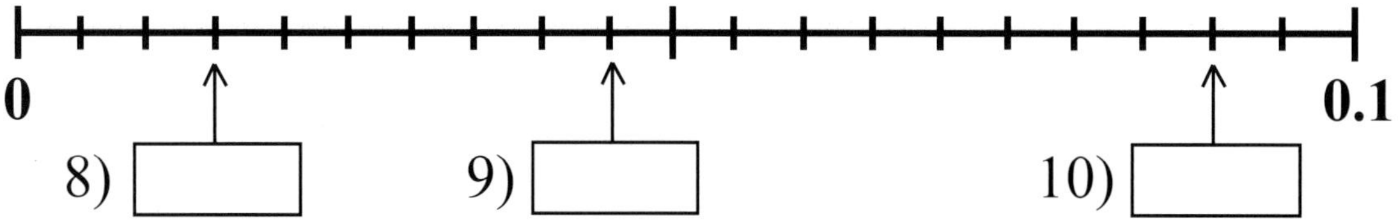

0

8)

9)

10)

0.1

# g. Rounding Decimal Values

By **Rounding off Decimals** we can find **Approximate answers**. We can round to a given number of Decimal Places.

Examples: | Round **3.135** and **3.134** to **2** Decimal Places.

**Example 1:**

2 Places | Decider

3.13|5

3.1**4**| Rounds up to **4**

- If the third decimal digit (Decider) is **5 or above**, it rounds up the digit before.

- The second decimal digit 3, is rounded up to **4**.

---

**Example 2:**

2 Places | Decider

3.13|4

3.1**3**| No rounding

- If the third decimal digit (Decider) is **4 or below**, it leaves the digit before it unchanged.

- The **3** remains the same.

---

## Exercise 3: 8  Round off the following:   **Score**

1) **3.615** to 2 d.p. ..........   2) **8.249** to 2 d.p. ..........

3) **13.14** to 1 d.p. ..........   4) **4.81** to 1 d.p. ...........

5) **1.151** to 1 d.p. ..........   6) **6.133** to 2 d.p. ..........

7) **2.2265** to 3 d.p. ..........   8) **7.641** to 2 d.p. ..........

9) **9.57** to 1 d.p. ..........   10) **5.7712** to 3 d.p. ..........

A complication can occur when a **9** has to be Rounded.

Example: | Round **2.195** to **2** Decimal Places. |

2 Places |   Decider

2.19**5**

    Rounds up to **2**

2.**20**

- The third digit **5** Rounds up the 9 to a **10** to give 2 tenths.
- In practise we **pass over the 9** dropping it down to 0.
  We then Round up the next digit.
  The 1 becomes a **2**.

Although the 0 in the hundredths column has no value here, it **must** be included as the question asked for **2 d.p.**

---

# Exercise 3: 9    Round off the following:   **Score** [ ]

1) **1.798** to 2 d.p. ..........  2) **5.2499** to 3 d.p. ..........

3) **16.993** to 1 d.p. ..........  4) **3.89** to 1 d.p. ..........

5) **7.194** to 2 d.p. ..........  6) **6.189** to 2 d.p. ..........

7) **2.2269** to 3 d.p. ..........  8) **3.6499** to 3 d.p. ..........

9) **7.599** to 1 d.p. ..........  10) **8.797** to 2 d.p. ..........

---

**Round Decimals to tenths, hundredths or thousandths.**
This is the same as rounding to **1**, **2** or **3** decimal places.
- Round to tenths means Round to **1** Decimal Place.
- Round to hundredths means Round to **2** Decimal Places.
- Round to thousandths means Round to **3** Decimal Places.

---

# Exercise 3: 10   Round to tenths, hundredths or thousandths:   **Score** [ ]

1) **0.72** (tenths) ..........  2) **3.459** (hundredths) ..........

3) **7.2754** (thousandths) ...........    4) **2.435** (hundredths) ...........

5) **4.283** (hundredths) ...........    6) **2.549** (tenths) ............

7) **0.8196** (thousandths) ...........    8) **6.468** (hundredths) ...........

9) **0.95** (tenths) ...........    10) **3.6438** (thousandths) ............

## Rounding Decimals to Whole Numbers.

If the digit after the decimal point is **5 or above** the unit rounds up. If it is **4 or below** it remains the same.

Example: Round **3.61** and **3.46** to Whole Numbers.

Note: The Decider is always the first digit after the Decimal Point.

Above 5 rounds up the whole number.

Below 5 leaves whole number the same.

**3.61** rounds to **4**     **3.46** rounds to **3**

## Exercise 3: 11   Round to Whole Numbers:

1) **0.81** ............    2) **6.468** ............

3) **17.2** ............    4) **3.649** ............

5) **0.99** ............    6) **2.47** ............

7) **20.7** ............    8) **9.874** ............

9) **8.64** ............    10) **5.17** ............

**Score**

# h. Significant Figures & Decimal Values

Numbers can also be rounded using **Significant Figures**. The first Significant Figure is always the first non-zero Digit which lies furthest to the left in the Number. This Digit is also the **most Significant** as it is the Digit with the greatest value.

The second most Significant Figure is the one directly to the right of this.

Example 1: $\boxed{5.41}$  Most Significant Figure = **5**
Second most Significant Figure = **4**
Third most Significant Figure = **1**

Example 2: $\boxed{0.105}$  Most Significant Figure = **1**
Second most Significant Figure = **0** (in the hundredths column)
Third most Significant Figure = **5**

Example 3: $\boxed{0.5103}$ The Significant Figures are **5103**

---

## Exercise 3: 12   Write the Significant Figures:

1)  **5,008**  ...............    2)  **0.00409**  ...............

3)  **7.906**  ...............    4)  **10.129**  ...............

5)  **0.409**  ...............    6)  **17.47**  ...............

7)  **3.088**  ...............    8)  **0.098**  ...............   **Score**

9)  **506**  ...............    10)  **0.109**  ...............

---

**Rounding or Correcting to several Significant Figures**.

Example 1:  Round off **73.39** to **3** significant figures.

Count 3 figures from the left.  Rounds up to **73.4**

Example 2:  Round off **0.001324** to **2** significant figures.

Ignore the zeros, but leave them in the answer.  **0.0013**

---

## Exercise 3: 13a   Round to Significant Figures.
1)  **1,004.7**  to **4** sig. fig.   ...............

2) **55.63** to **3** sig. fig.             3) **908.8** to **3** sig. fig.

.............                                .............

4) **32.7** to **2** sig. fig.              5) **0.099** to **1** sig. fig.

.............                                .............

Example 3: | **8,290** correct to **1** significant figure. |

The cut off is at **8ǀ290**.  No rounding up is needed, so write **8**.
Fill in the columns up to the Decimal Point with zeros. **8,000** (Ans)

Example 4: | **2,976** correct to **2** significant figures. |

The Cut off is at **29ǀ76**.  Round to **30**, then fill in the
columns up to the Decimal Point with zeros.     **3,000** (Ans)

## Exercise 3: 13b      Round to Significant Figures.

6)  **12,375** to **2** sig. fig.           7)  **5,011** to **3** sig. fig.

.............                                .............

8)  **50,766** to **3** sig. fig.           9)  **384** to **2** sig. fig.

.............                                .............        **Score**

10)  **6,880** to **1** sig. fig.  .............

# *i.* Estimates and Approximations

**Estimating** is a good way of checking answers.
- Round to 'easy' numbers like **10, 100** or **1,000**.
- Work out the Estimate using these numbers.
- Use the symbol ≈ which means 'nearly equal to'.
- **Right Order of Magnitude** means about the right size.

(The Magnitude of something is a measurement of its size.)

Example 1: | Estimate $63.88 - 2.9^2$ |

$$63.88 - 2.9^2 \longrightarrow 64 - 3^2 \longrightarrow 64 - 9 \approx 55$$

Round the Decimals          Multiply out the          Subtract
to the nearest unit.        Square number.            as normal.

If the number is very small it is Approximated to zero.

Example 2: | Estimate **109.7 + 0.0003** |

$$109.7 + 0.0003 \longrightarrow 110 + 0 \approx 110$$

Round the Decimals to units of 10.

(Numbers with a difference of less than 10% would usually be considered to be in the same Order of Magnitude.)

---

**Exercise 3: 14**  Estimate to nearest whole number:  **Score**

1) $4.7 + 8.9 \approx$ .......... 2) $119.55 - 69.81 \approx$ ..........

3) $95.26 \times 6.3 \approx$ .......... 4) $600.1 \div 9.8 \approx$ ..........

5) $3.1^2 + 6.9 \approx$ .......... 6) $16.44 - 9.11 \approx$ ..........

7) $7.26 \times 10.8 \approx$ .......... 8) $60.22 \div 5.4 \approx$ ..........

9) $5.1 \times 8.62 \approx$ .......... 10) $5.9^2 \div 6.2 \approx$ ..........

# 3. Addition and Subtraction

The rules of **Addition** and **Subtraction**.

1. Keep the Decimal Point in line.
2. Fill all the empty spaces with zeros to make a box.
3. Add or Subtract as normal.

Example 1: | **5.41 + 62.9** |   Example 2: | **35.4 − 5.25** |

$$
\begin{array}{r}
0\,5.4\,1 \\
6\,2.9\,0\,+ \\
\hline
6\,8.3\,1 \\
\end{array}
\qquad
\begin{array}{r}
3\,5.{}^{3}\cancel{4}{}^{1}0 \\
0\,5.2\,5\,- \\
\hline
3\,0.1\,5 \\
\end{array}
$$

# Exercise 3: 15    Set out and calculate. Do not Round:

1)  **8.3 + 6.5 =** ..........       2)  **12.1 + 0.83 =** ..........

3)  **12.3 − 7.4 =** ..........       4)  **16.5 − 8.63 =** ..........

5)  **31.13 + 17 + 0.016**       6)  **5.12 − 0.597 =** ..........
     **=** ..........

7)  **33.45 − 6.856**       8)  **6.01 + 0.695 =** ..........
     **=** ..........

9)  **215.07 − 108.78**       10)  **28.714 − 16.45**
     **=** ..........                          **=** ..........

Score

# 4. Multiplication

## a. Decimal Multiplication

For Decimal Multiplication leave out the Decimal Point whilst doing the sum and replace it after completion.

**Example:**

1. Leave out the Decimal Points when Multiplying.

$$\boxed{18.3 \times 0.41}$$

The zero on **041** is now irrelevant; it becomes **41**.

This becomes **1 8 3** $\times$ **4 1**

2. Proceed as a normal Multiplication.

Using the **Italian Method**
Multiply  **1** $\times$ **183** = **183**
Put a **zero** in the second row.
Multiply  **4** $\times$ **183** = **7320**
Add   **183** + **7320** = **7503**

$$
\begin{array}{r}
1\,8\,3 \\
4\,1 \times \\
\hline
1\,8\,3 \\
7\,3\,2\,0 \\
\hline
7\,5\,0\,3
\end{array}
$$

3. Count the Digits after the Decimal Points in both the original numbers.

$$1 \quad + \quad 2 \;=\; 3 \text{ digits}$$

$$1\,8\,.\,3 \times 0\,.\,4\,1$$

4. Add the number of Digits together after the Decimal Points.

$$1 + 2 = 3 \text{ digits}$$

5. Count three places from the right in the answer and replace the Decimal Point.

Count in the point 3 places from the right.

$$7\,.\,5\,0\,3$$

# Exercise 3: 16  Round (where necessary) to two Decimal Places:

1)   **2.3 × 8 =** ............   2)   **9.4 × 0.7 =** ..........

3)   **8.6 × 5 =** .........   4)   **9.4 × 0.03 =** .........

5)   **0.4 × 0.4 =** .........   6)   **2.9 × 1.8 =** .........

7)   **0.43 × 2.5 =** .........   8)   **24.44 × 4.4 =** .........

9)   **3.9 × 1.2 =** .........   10)   **0.7 × 0.05 =** .........

**Score**

# b. Multiplying Decimals by Tens

**Multiplying by ten** moves the Decimal Point **one place to the right**. Each Multiplication by ten takes the Decimal Point one place further to the right.

Example: | Multiply **0.3 × 10** and **0.3 × 100**

These sums can be written:

Multiply by **10**
• move d.p. one place.

1 place right
→
$$0.30 \times 10 = 03.0 = 3$$

Multiply by **100**
• move d.p. two places.

2 places right
→
$$0.30 \times 100 = 030.0 = 30$$

To assist in counting the point it helps to <u>Add zeros</u>.

Add
zeros
**0.300** becomes **030.0**      moves 2 places right.

---

## Exercise 3: 17 Multiply the following:   Score

1) $2.5 \times 10 =$ .........

2) $3.62 \times 10 =$ .........

3) $94.32 \times 100 =$ .........

4) $2.3 \times 100 =$ .........

5) $16 \times 10 =$ .........

6) $63.18 \times 10 =$ .........

7) $32.653 \times 100 =$ .........

8) $4.3 \times 1,000 =$ .........

9) $0.7 \times 100 =$ .........

10) $23.47 \times 1,000 =$ .........

# 5. Division
## a. Decimal Division
### (i). Dividing by a Whole Number

Dividing into a Decimal by a Whole Number follows the same principles as ordinary Division without Remainders.

Example: $\boxed{5.1 \div 12 \text{ (Round to 2 Decimal Places)}}$.

$$
\begin{array}{r}
0.425 \\
12\,\overline{\smash{\big)}\,5.100} \\
4\,8\phantom{00} \\
\overline{\phantom{0}30\phantom{0}} \\
24\phantom{0} \\
\overline{\phantom{00}60} \\
60 \\
\overline{00}
\end{array}
$$

**0.43 (ans)**

Do not put Remainders at the end of a Decimal Division.

Add some zeros to enable the Division to continue.

Keep the Decimal Point in the answer, directly above where the Decimal Point is in the question.

Work out 3 Decimal places and then round to 2 Decimal places.

Follow the same technique for Short and Long Division.

---

**Remainders** and **Decimals** are not the same:

A **Remainder** is a Whole Number that is left over.

This is **2 groups of 6 units and 3 units left over.**

Example: $\boxed{15 \div 6}$

$$
\begin{array}{r}
2 \text{ rem. } 3 \\
6\,\overline{\smash{\big)}\,15}
\end{array}
$$

A **Decimal** is obtained by carrying the remainder into the tenths column. It is then Divided to give tenths.

This is **2 groups of 6 units and 5 tenths of 6.**
(5 tenths of the Divisor [Divider] which is 6.)

Example: $\boxed{15 \div 6}$

$$
\begin{array}{r}
2.5 \\
6\,\overline{\smash{\big)}\,15.{}^{3}0}
\end{array}
$$

# Exercise 3: 18a    Divide the following:

(Questions 1-2 Divide exactly to 1 or 2 Decimal Places)

1)    $33.3 \div 3$        2)    $23.4 \div 5$

$$3\,\overline{)\,3\,3\,.\,3}$$        $$5\,\overline{)\,2\,3\,.\,4\,0}$$

=  ..............        =  ..............

(Round each answer to **2 Decimal Places** in questions 3-4)

3)    $6.36 \div 15$        4)    $90.4 \div 25$

=  ..............        =  ..............

(Round each answer to **3 Decimal Places** in questions 5-6)

5)    $0.1974 \div 21$        6)    $0.971 \div 13$

=  ..............        =  ..............

## (ii). Recurring Decimals

Some numbers that will not Divide exactly will produce a Recurring Decimal. This is a number that has a repeated pattern that will go on the same way forever.

Example 1:  $\boxed{17.2 \div 6}$        Divide the Decimal the same way as before.

  

$$6\,)\overline{17.^{5}2^{4}0^{4}0^{4}0} = 2.8666$$

The answer can be shown with a Recurring Dot.

$$2.8\dot{6}$$

It can also be Rounded to 2 d.p. **2.87**

Sometimes two different digits repeat over and over again.

Example 2: $6.84 \div 11$

$$11\,)\overline{6.^{6}8^{2}4^{2}0^{9}0^{2}0^{9}0} = 0.621818$$

The answer can be shown with two Recurring Dots.

$$0.62\dot{1}\dot{8}$$

## Exercise 3: 18b    Calculate using Recurring Dots:

7) $5.2 \div 3$

$$3\,)\overline{5.200}$$

= ...............

8) $31.6 \div 9$

$$9\,)\overline{31.60}$$

= ...............

9) $100 \div 18$

= ...............

10) $33.7 \div 33$

= ...............

Score ☐

## (iii). Dividing by a Decimal

In Decimal Division, the Dividing Number (Divisor) must be a Whole Number. If the Divisor is a Decimal:

1. Move the Decimal Point in the number you are Dividing by (Divisor), to the right, making it a Whole Number.

2. Compensate by moving the Decimal Point in the
   number you are Dividing into (the Dividend), to the
   right by the same number of places.

Example: $1.73 \div 0.7$

Move 1 place    Move 1 place

$1.73 \div 0.7$

$17.3 \div 7$

Move the Decimal Point one place to the right on the Divisor and Dividend.

This is now **17.3** Divided by **7** units.

$$
\begin{array}{r}
2.471 \\
7\overline{)17.3^3 0^5 0^1}
\end{array}
$$

Add some zeros to enable the Division to continue.

**2.47**    Rounded to 2 Decimal Places.

Follow the same technique for Short and Long Division.

## Exercise 3: 19    Divide the following:

(Questions 1-4 Divide exactly to two Decimal Places.)

1)    $7.64 \div 0.8$

$$8\overline{)76.40}$$

=  ...............

3)    $52.86 \div 1.2$

2)    $9.71 \div 0.04$

$$4\overline{)971.00}$$

=  ...............

4)    $88.2 \div 2.4$

=  ...............

=  ...............

(Use a **Recurring Dot** to show Recurring Decimals in questions 5-6.)

    5)    **65.8 ÷ 0.06**       6)    **52.5 ÷ 0.9**




       = ...............         = ...............

(Round each answer to **2 Decimal Places** in questions 7-8.)

    7)    **65.35 ÷ 1.3**      8)    **87.5 ÷ 0.16**




       = ...............         = ...............

(Round each answer to **3 Decimal Places** in questions 9-10.)

    9)    **576.7 ÷ 1.4**     10)    **4.892 ÷ 0.17**




       = ...............         = ...............   **Score**

## (iv). Hidden Decimals

There are no Decimals in the question, but they appear in the answer. Therefore the Decimal is hidden.

Example: $15 \div 4$ — No Decimal Points are evident.

$$4 \overline{\smash{)}15.^30^20} = 3.75$$

Add zeros to continue the Division.

**3.75** — The answer gives two Decimal Places.

---

**Exercise 3: 20**  Divide the following:  **Score** 

Answer to 2 Decimal Places where necessary.

1)  $9 \div 2 = $ ..........

$$2 \overline{\smash{)}9.0}$$

2)  $7 \div 6 = $ ..........

$$6 \overline{\smash{)}7.00}$$

3)  $19 \div 5 = $ ..........

4)  $22 \div 6 = $ ..........

5)  $110 \div 4 = $ ..........

6)  $21 \div 5 = $ ..........

7)  $12 \div 7 = $ ..........

8)  $81 \div 8 = $ ..........

9)  $51 \div 9 = $ ..........

10)  $40 \div 7 = $ ..........

# b. Dividing Decimals by Tens

**Dividing by ten** moves the Decimal Point **one place to the left**. Each Division by ten takes the Decimal Point one place further to the left.

Example: | Divide $0.3 \div 10$ and $0.3 \div 100$

These sums can be written:

Divide by 10
• move d.p one place.

1 place left

$$0.3 \div 10 = 0.03$$

Divide by 100
• move d.p. two places.

2 places left

$$0.3 \div 100 = 0.003$$

To assist in counting the point it helps to <u>Add zeros</u>.

Add zeros → $000.3$ becomes $0.003$  moves 2 places left.

---

## Exercise 3: 21    Divide the following:    Score

1) $38.6 \div 10 =$ ..........

2) $23.6 \div 100 =$ ..........

3) $19 \div 10 =$ ..........

4) $95 \div 100 =$ ..........

5) $7.45 \div 100 =$ ..........

6) $16.5 \div 10 =$ ..........

7) $12.9 \div 100 =$ ..........

8) $12.8 \div 1,000 =$ ..........

9) $25.6 \div 100 =$ ..........

10) $0.6 \div 100 =$ ..........

# 6. Decimal Operations
## a. Decimal Tables

Decimal Tables work in the same way as Addition, Subtraction, Multiplication and Division Tables, except Decimal values are used (see earlier in **Book 1**).

**Exercise 3: 22** Find the missing amounts: **Score**

1-2)

A = .........

B = .........

| + | 1.2 | 2.4 |
|---|---|---|
| A | 2.3 | 3.5 |
| 3.7 | 4.9 | B |

3-4)

A = .........

B = .........

| − | 10 | 14.5 |
|---|---|---|
| A | 6.4 | 10.9 |
| 3.9 | 6.1 | B |

5-7)

A = .........

B = .........

C = .........

| × | 0.9 | 0.3 | A |
|---|---|---|---|
| 6 | B | 1.8 | 2.4 |
| 4 | 3.6 | 1.2 | 1.6 |
| 3 | 2.7 | C | 1.2 |

8-10)

A = .........

B = .........

C = .........

| ÷ | A | 16 | 20 |
|---|---|---|---|
| 5 | 2.4 | B | 4 |
| 3 | 4 | 5.3̇ | 6.6̇ |
| C | 8 | 10.6̇ | 13.3̇ |

## b. Order of Operations
### i. With Brackets

If a question contains Brackets, do the sum in the Brackets first.

Example: $8.82 \div (4.68 - 1.08)$

Brackets first $4.68 - 1.08 = 3.6$ then $8.82 \div 3.6 = 2.45$

**Exercise 3: 23a** Calculate the following to 2 d.p.:

1) $0.207 \div (1.5 \times 0.6)$

= ...............

2) $(2.9 + 0.56) \times 2.5$

= ...............

3) $(0.59 \times 0.7) + 4.25$

= ...............

4) $5.5 \div (0.12 - 0.035)$

= ...............

5) $0.16 \times (9.3 - 1.25) =$ ...............

## ii. Without Brackets

The order of operations can be remembered by using the acronym **B I D M A S** (sometimes seen as **B O D M A S**).

**B**rackets, **I**ndices, **D**ivision, **M**ultiplication, **A**ddition and **S**ubtraction
or **O**f (to the power 'of')

If a sum has no Brackets or Indices but has two or more signs then do $\div$ or $\times$ first (in the order of the question), then $+$ or $-$ (in the order of the question).

Example: $\boxed{4.9 - 0.5 \times 0.8}$

Multiply first $0.5 \times 0.8 = 0.4$ then $4.9 - 0.4 = \mathbf{4.5}$

**Exercise 3: 23b** Calculate the following to 2 d.p.:

6) $1.2 + 4.5 - 0.6$

= ...............

7) $2.2 + 0.12 \times 6.3$

= ...............

8) $4.6 - 0.3 + 4.25$

= ...............

9) $8.6 \div 4.5 - 0.85$

= ...............

10) $0.14 \times 4.3 \div 1.5 =$ ...............

Score [ ]

# 7. Decimal Problems

Remember the following **Definitions**:

| | |
|---|---|
| Add → **Sum** | Subtract → **Difference** |
| Multiply → **Product** | Divide → **Quotient** |

## Exercise 3: 24   Do the following Calculatons:

**Score**

1) Find the **Sum** of
46.78  and  5.69

................

2) Find the **Difference**
between **78.2**  and  **9.9**

................

3) Find the **Product** of
56  and  6.9

................

4) Find the **Quotient** of
14.3  by  2.6

................

This table shows the marks scored by three children in their end of year tests.

| Subject | Paula | Vishal | Naomi |
|---|---|---|---|
| Maths | 46.3 | 27 | 33.5 |
| English | 32.5 | 37. 9 | 38.8 |
| Science | 40.6 | 40.5 | 47.6 |

5) Who scored the lowest score in any subject? ...............

6) What was the highest score achieved in any subject?

................

7) Which child has scored the most overall?  ...............

8) Who has scored the least overall?  ...............

9) Find the Sum of **44.3**  and  **2.9**  then Divide it by the Difference between  **6.2**  and  **8.5**. Give your answer to 2 d.p.  ...............

10) Find the Difference between  **2.7**  and  **3.1**  then Multiply it by  **6.7**  ...............

# Answers

## Chapter One
## Basic Number

### Exercise 1: 1
1) 35  2) 409  3) 100,000
4) 446  5) 6,021  6) 75,000
7) 965,000  8) 1,400,000
9) 949  10) 152,395

### Exercise 1: 2
1) Eleven  2) Twenty three
3) Eight hundred and ninety
nine
4) One hundred and ninety
5) Three hundred and fifty nine
6) One thousand, three
hundred and ten
7) Twenty five thousand,
eight hundred and fifty three
8) Sixty nine thousand, nine
hundred and forty two
9) Two hundred and thirty
four thousand, three hundred
10) One million, five hundred
and forty five thousand,
seven hundred and seventy

### Exercise 1:3
1) 9,990; 9,078; 5,743,
3,561; 1,232; 772
2) Fifty; Eight
3) 600; 50; 50,000
4) 376,216  5) 79,433
6) 987; 978; 897; 879,
798; 789
7) 516,998  8) 11,210
9) 12; 88; 901; 1,192;
7,069; 8,754
10) 13,589

### Exercise 1: 4a
1) 11,553  2) 9,441
3) 6,768  4) 13,622
### Exercise 1:4b
(Missing numbers only)
5) 7; 5; 6  6) 8; 1; 8

7) 2; 1; 9  8) 7; 9; 8
9) 4; 6; 3  10) 1; 5; 0

### Exercise 1: 5a
1) 2,233  2) 7,767
3) 1,338  4) 5,815
### Exercise 1:5b
5) 163  6) 187
7) 1,521  8) 1,527
9) 2,801  10) 2,506

### Exercise 1: 6
1) 322  2) 88  3) 208
4) 2,371  5) 1,273  6) 1,401
7) 2,754  8) 6,482
9) 31,388  10) 28,013

### Exercise 1: 7
(Missing numbers only)
1) 8; 2; 1  2) 5; 2; 6
3) 0; 3; 6  4) 5; 9; 5
5) 4; 0; 1; 6  6) 2; 3; 9; 3
7) 8; 4; 1; 1  8) 1; 2; 4; 5
9) 3; 0; 9; 2  10) 7; 7; 0; 7

### Exercise 1: 8a
1) 20,796  2) 21,988
3) 29,935  4) 47,706
5) 52,640  6) 78,888
### Exercise 1: 8b
(Missing numbers only)
7) 2; 1  8) 8; 3
9) 7; 8 or 2;4  10) 9; 2

### Exercise 1: 9
1) 50  2) 600  3) 7,000
4) 2,500  5) 300  6) 10,000
7) 15,000  8) 55,000
9) 1,300  10) 50,000

### Exercise 1: 10
1) 805  2) 4,365  3) 1,083
4) 1,075  5) 12,070
6) 6,408  7) 37,050
8) 17,504  9) 104,312
10) 161,025

### Exercise 1: 11
1) 612  2) 3,066
3) 2,666  4) 1,456
5) 77,004  6) 66,148
7) 11,025  8) 230,007
9) 405,246  10) 638,172

### Exercise 1: 12a
1) 86  2) 94
3) 98  4) 1,631 r. 2
5) 989 r. 3  6) 9,717 r. 1
### Exercise 1: 12b
(Missing numbers only)
7) 2  8) 3  9) 4  10) 4

### Exercise 1: 13
1) 5  2) 3  3) 50  4) 56
5) 2  6) 320  7) 40
8) 52  9) 60  10) 59

### Exercise 1: 14
1) 654  2) 689  3) 321
4) 412  5) 271 r. 7
6) 301 r. 7  7) 683 r. 11
8) 936 r. 11  9) 581 r. 12
10) 954 r. 4

### Exercise 1: 15
1) 1080  2) 45  3) 55
4) 46  5) 52  6) 19
7) 74  8) 54  9) 2  10) 4

### Exercise 1: 16
1-2) 119; 64
3-5) 48; 127; 79
6-7) 1,462; 43
8-10) 1,296; 48; 27

### Exercise 1: 17a
1) 32  2) 7  3) 21
4) 130  5) 4
### Exercise 1: 17b
6) 43  7) 15  8) 53
9) 21  10) 137

# Answers

## Exercise 1: 18a
1) 5      2) 48    3) 54
4) 189   5) 141

## Exercise 1: 18b
6) 50    7) 96    8) 24
9) 35    10) 8

## Exercise 1: 19
1) 7, 9, 8, 2     2) 173 r.7
3) 5,600,000    4) 172,924
5) 14   6) 182   7) 167
8) 15,665  9) 90  10) 139

## Chapter Two
## Number
## Relationships

## Exercise 2: 1
1) A = 9  2)  A = 3
3-4)  A = 19 ; B = 16
5-6)  A = 12 ; B = 18
7-8)  A = 10 ; B = 9
9-10) A = 20 ; B = 80

## Exercise 2: 2
1-2)   A = 10; B = 17
3-4)   A = 5; B = 4
5-7)   A = 7; B = 10; C = 20
8-10)  A = 6; B = 8; C = 21

## Exercise 2: 3
1-2)   A = 4; B = 11
3-4)   A = 5; B = 3
5-7)   A = 12; B = 21; C = 0
8-10)  A = 5; B = 9; C = 6

## Exercise 2: 4
1-2)   A = 30;  B = 10
3-4)   A = 81;  B = 4
5-7)   A = 7;    B = 35
       C = 6
8-10)  A = 3;    B = 28
       C = 6

## Exercise 2: 5
1-2)   A = 6;   B = 3
3-4)   A = 12;  B = 2

5-7)   A = 72; B = 4; C = 12
8-10)  A – 45; B – 18; C – 9

## Exercise 2: 6
1)  19,107      2)  833
3)  1848        4)  21,775
5)  5,445       6)  50,505
7)  30,409      8)  41,925
9)  19,491      10)  2,706

## Exercise 2: 7
1)  7,182       2)  585
3)  2,964       4)  27,772
5)  3,588       6)  51,282
7)  11,628      8)  17,595
9)  19,701      10)  3,196

## Exercise 2: 8a
1)  5,977       2)  2,695
3)  10,604      4)  12,312
5)  24,308

## Exercise 2: 8b
6)  19 r.6      7)  17 r.18
8)  11 r.46     9)  19 r.50
10) 23 r.25

## Exercise 2: 9
1) 30  2) 560  3) 300
4) 200  5) 3,000  6) 6,000
7) 90  8) 150  9) 150  10) 30

## Exercise 2: 10
1) Odd   2) Even   3) Odd
4) Even  5) Odd    6) Odd
7) Even  8) Even
9) 82, 866, 800, 54
10) 1,989 does not

## Exercise 2: 11
1) 16    2) 49    3) 81
4) 144   5) 36    6) 256
7) 225   8) 289   9) 625
10) 324

## Exercise 2: 12
1) 2   2) 5   3) 10   4) 4
5) 6   6) 8   7) 7   8) 11
9) 9   10) 12

## Exercise 2: 13
1) 8   2) 64   3) 216
4) 343  5) 125  6) 729
7) 1,000  8) 512
9) 1,728  10) 1,331

## Exercise 2: 14
1) 4   2) 5   3) 2   4) 8
5) 6   6) 10  7) 3   8) 9
9) 7   10) 11

## Exercise 2: 15
1) 16  2) 1  3) 81  4) 625
5) 729  6) 64  7) 243
8) 1,024  9) 3,125  10) 256

## Exercise 2: 16
1)  Not prime 2)  Prime
3)  Not prime 4)  Prime
5)  Prime  6)  Not prime
7)  Prime  8)  Not Prime
9)  Prime  10) Not prime

## Exercise 2: 17
1) Yes  2) No   3) Yes
4) Yes  5) Yes  6) Yes
7) 24  8) 45  9) 72  10) 12

## Exercise 2: 18
1)  15   2)  36   3)  28
4)  55   5)  45   6)  21
7)  10 and 15
8)  6 and 10 or 15 and 1
9)  3 and 6
10) 10 and 21 or 3 and 28

## Exercise 2: 19a
1)  19, 10  2)  54, 162
3)  29, 35  4)  12, 30
5)  125, 216  6)  6, 0

## Exercise 2: 19b
7)  32, 64     8)  12, 15
9)  8, 7       10) 25, 36

# Answers



## Exercise 2: 20
1-2) 40, 140
3-4) 100, 350
5-7) 60, 180, 340
8-10) 14, 56, 112

## Exercise 2: 21a
1) 9  2) 3  3) -1$^{\circ}$C  4) -5$^{\circ}$C  5) 10$^{\circ}$C
## Exercise 2: 21b
6) a) -3 < 2  b) -8 < 10
   c) 2 > -7
7) -10, -5, -2, -1, 5, 8, 10
## Exercise 2: 21c
8) 4  9) 1  10) -7

## Exercise 2: 22
1) 1, 3, 5, 9, 15, 45
2) 1, 2 ,4, 5, 10, 20
3) 1, 3, 5, 15  4) 1, 13
5) 1, 2, 3, 6, 9, 18
6) 1, 2, 13, 26  7) 1, 5, 25
8) 1, 2, 3, 5, 6, 10, 15, 30
9) 1, 2, 5, 10, 25, 50
10) 1, 2, 3, 4, 6, 8, 12, 16, 24, 48

## Exercise 2: 23a
1) 2, 3, 6  2) 1, 2, 4, 8
3) 3, 6  4) 3, 5, 15
## Exercise 2: 23b
5) 1  6) 7  7) 4  8) 8
9) 4  10) 12

## Exercise 2: 24
1) 2, 5  2) 3, 5  3) 2, 5
4) 2, 7  5) 2, 13  6) 2, 3  7) 3
8) 2  9) 5  10) 2

## Exercise 2: 25
1) 14, 21, 28, 35, 42
2) 16, 24, 32, 40, 48
3) 30, 45, 60, 75, 90
4) 18, 27, 36, 45, 54
5) 32, 48, 64, 80, 96
6) 28, 42, 56, 70, 84
7) 24, 36, 48, 60, 72
8) 12, 18, 24, 30, 36
9) 26, 39, 52, 65, 78
10) 22, 33, 44, 55, 66

## Exercise 2: 26a
1) 12, 24  2) 36, 48
3) 12, 18  4) 24, 48
## Exercise 2: 26b
5) 24  6) 36  7) 72
8) 42  9) 56  10) 132

## Exercise 2: 27
1) 53 seats  2) 97 do not
3) No  4) 7 shelves
5) 566 seats  6) 20 passengers
7) 2 classrooms  8) 390 children
9) 210 books  10) 55 children

## Exercise 2: 28
1) 24  2) 290  3) 409
4) 526  5) 1,009  6) 740
7) 1,321  8) 1,854  9) 2,155
10) 958

## Exercise 2: 29
1) XXXIII  2) LXVII
3) CDLXXVIII  4) XCIX
5) CCXLII  6) DXXIX
7) DCCLXXXIV
8) MCDXLIV
9) MMCDXCVIII
10) MMMCMLIX

## Exercise 2: 30
1a) A = 17; B = 11
 b) A = 42; B = 18
2a) 196  b) 128  c) 1296  d) 13
3a) 4, 6, 8, 9, 10  b) 6 and 10
 c) 23  d) 16
4a) 25, 36  b) 46, 81
5a) 7  b) -3  c) 0
6a) 1, 2, 4, 8, 16, 32, 64
 b) 18  c) 2, 3, 5  d) 7
7a) 60  b) 168  c) 70
8) 480 bottles  9) 756 glasses
10) 850 seats

## Chapter Three
## Decimals
## Exercise 3: 1
1) 6.0  2) 71.0
3) 59.0  4) 566.0
5) 4,988.0  6) 9
7) 98  8) 12
9) 812  10) 5,234

## Exercise 3: 2

|     | TH | H | T | U | t | h | th |
|-----|----|---|---|---|---|---|----|
| 1)  |    |   | 3 | 4 | 1 | 2 |    |
| 2)  |    |   |   | 0 | 1 | 2 | 9  |
| 3)  |    | 6 | 6 | 7 | 2 |   |    |
| 4)  |    |   | 1 | 0 | 3 | 4 | 6  |
| 5)  | 1  | 9 | 7 | 5 | 0 | 2 | 1  |
| 6)  |    |   |   | 1 | 8 |   |    |
| 7)  |    |   |   | 8 | 6 | 5 |    |
| 8)  |    |   |   | 0 | 9 | 9 | 1  |
| 9)  |    | 7 | 7 | 7 | 4 | 4 |    |
| 10) | 1  | 0 | 8 | 7 | 0 | 5 | 1  |

## Exercise 3: 3
1) 6 tenths  2) 3 units
3) 9 tenths
4) 2 hundredths
5) 3 thousandths
6) 7 thousandths
7) 0.012  8) 1.67
9) 4.21  10) 0.322

## Exercise 3: 4
1) 661 thousandths
2) 112 hundredths
3) 4 tens, 1 unit, 3 tenths
   and 2 hundredths
4) 5 units and 78
   hundredths
5) 66 units and 728
   thousandths
6) 15 thousandths
7) 7,901 hundredths
8) 8 units and 72
   hundredths
9) 1,058 tenths
10) 69 tenths

# Answers

## Exercise 3: 5
1) 1.09; 1.306; 1.6
2) 0.001; 0.01; 0.1
3) 0.55; 1.21; 3.8
4) 0.1; 0.99; 1.9
5) 1.213; 1.33; 1.4
6) 2.9; 3.71; 3.8
7) 3; 2.9; 2.13
8) 1.2; 1.102; 1.012
9) 14.1; 1.141, 0.41
10) 0.91; 0.81; 0.723

## Exercise 3: 6
1) 0.04 < 3.2
2) 0.167 < 0.2
3) 1.07 > 0.157
4) 54.158 < 54.185
5) 1.058 < 1.06
6) 2.018 > 2.009
7) 0.6 > 0.47
8) 0.03 > 0.027
9) 5.19 > 3.599
10) 0.076 < 0.11

## Exercise 3: 7
1) 0.04  2) 0.09  3) 0.2
4) 0.55  5) 0.85  6) 0.003
7) 0.008  8) 0.015
9) 0.045  10) 0.09

## Exercise 3: 8
1) 3.62  2) 8.25  3) 13.1
4) 4.8  5) 1.2  6) 6.13
7) 2.227  8) 7.64  9) 9.6
10) 5.771

## Exercise 3: 9
1) 1.80  2) 5.250  3) 17.0
4) 3.9  5) 7.19  6) 6.19
7) 2.227  8) 3.650  9) 7.6
10) 8.80

## Exercise 3: 10
1) 0.7  2) 3.46  3) 7.275
4) 2.44  5) 4.28  6) 2.5
7) 0.820  8) 6.47  9) 1.0
10) 3.644

## Exercise 3: 11
1) 1  2) 6  3) 17  4) 4
5) 1  6) 2  7) 21  8) 10
9) 9  10) 5

## Exercise 3: 12
1) 5008  2) 409  3) 7906
4) 10129  5) 409  6) 1747
7) 3088  8) 98  9) 506
10) 109

## Exercise 3: 13a
1) 1,005  2) 55.6  3) 909
4) 33  5) 0.1

## Exercise 3: 13b
6) 12,000  7) 5,010
8) 50,800  9) 380  10) 7,000

## Exercise 3: 14
1) 14  2) 50  3) 570  4) 60
5) 16  6) 7  7) 77  8) 12
9) 45  10) 6

## Exercise 3: 15
1) 14.8  2) 12.93
3) 4.9  4) 7.87
5) 48.146  6) 4.523
7) 26.594  8) 6.705
9) 106.29  10) 12.264

## Exercise 3: 16
1) 18.4  2) 6.58  3) 43
4) 0.28  5) 0.16  6) 5.22
7) 1.08  8) 107.54
9) 4.68  10) 0.04

## Exercise 3: 17
1) 25  2) 36.2  3) 9432
4) 230  5) 160  6) 631.8
7) 3265.3  8) 4,300
9) 70  10) 23,470

## Exercise 3: 18a
1) 11.1  2) 4.68
3) 0.42  4) 3.62
5) 0.009  6) 0.075

## Exercise 3: 18b
7) $1.7\dot{3}$  8) $3.5\dot{1}$
9) $5.\dot{5}$  10) $1.02\dot{1}$

## Exercise 3: 19
1) 9.55  2) 242.75
3) 44.05  4) 36.75
5) $1,096.\dot{6}$  6) $58.\dot{3}$
7) 50.27  8) 546.88
9) 411.929  10) 28.776

## Exercise 3: 20
1) 4.5  2) 1.17
3) 3.8  4) 3.67
5) 27.5  6) 4.2
7) 1.71  8) 10.13
9) 5.67  10) 5.71

## Exercise 3: 21
1) 3.86  2) 0.236
3) 1.9  4) 0.95
5) 0.0745  6) 1.65
7) 0.129  8) 0.0128
9) 0.256  10) 0.006

## Exercise 3: 22
1) A = 1.1  2) B = 6.1
3) A = 3.6  4) B = 10.6
5) A = 0.4  6) B = 5.4
7) C = 0.9  8) A = 12
9) B = 3.2  10) C = 1.5

## Exercise 3: 23a
1) 0.23  2) 8.65  3) 4.66
4) 64.71  5) 1.29

## Exercise 3: 23b
6) 5.10  7) 2.96  8) 8.55
9) 1.06  10) 0.40

## Exercise 3: 24
1) 52.47  2) 68.3
3) 386.4  4) 5.5
5) Vishal scored lowest
6) 47.6 in Science
7) Naomi scored most
8) Vishal scored least
9) 20.52  10) 2.68

# PROGRESS CHARTS



## 1. BASIC NUMBER

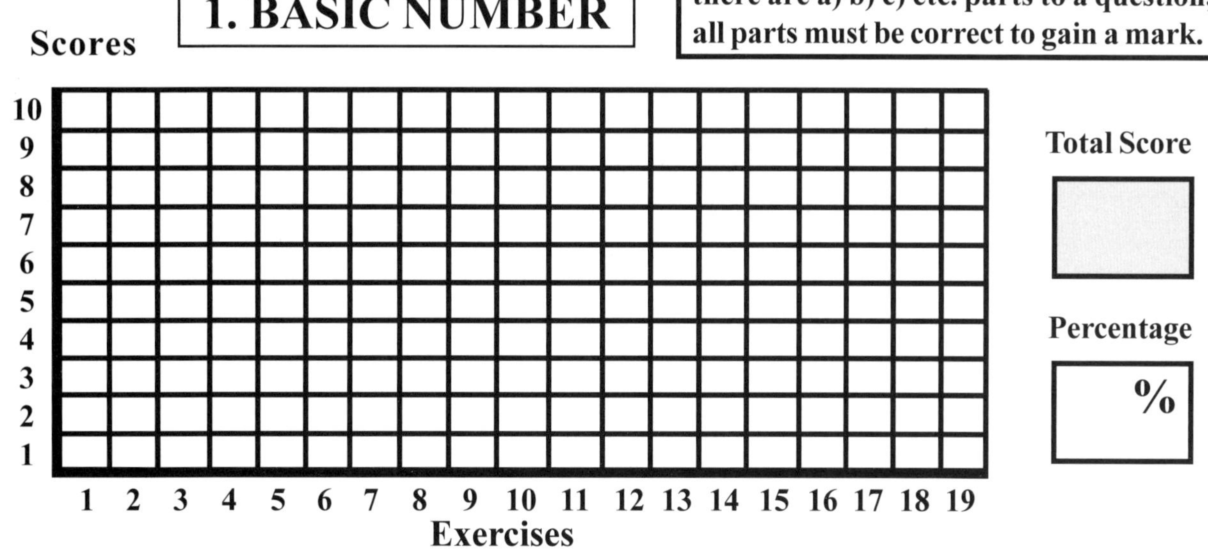


## 2. NUMBER RELATIONSHIPS

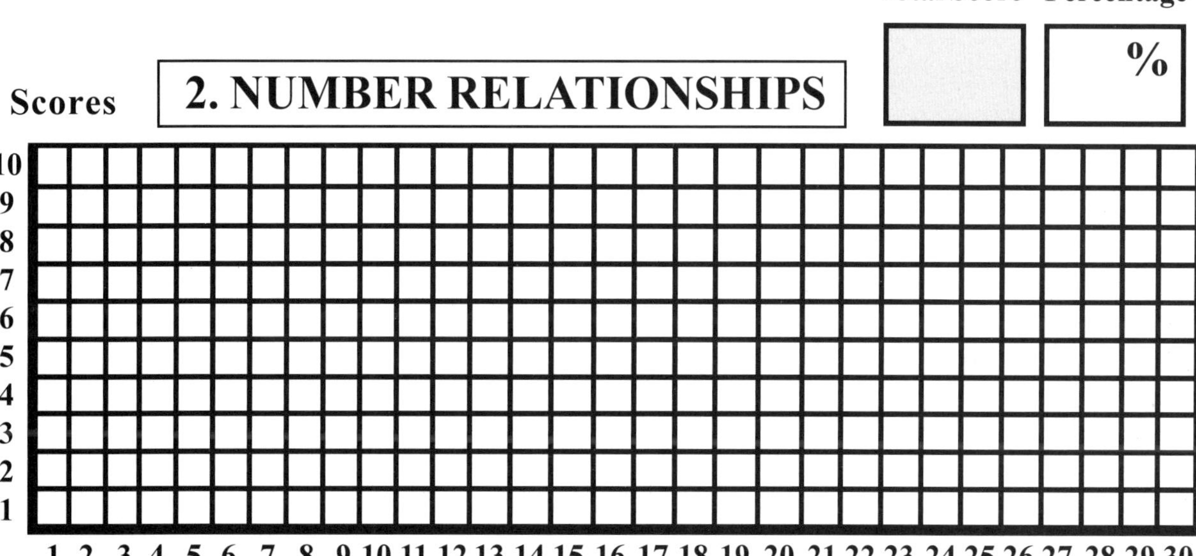


## 3. DECIMALS

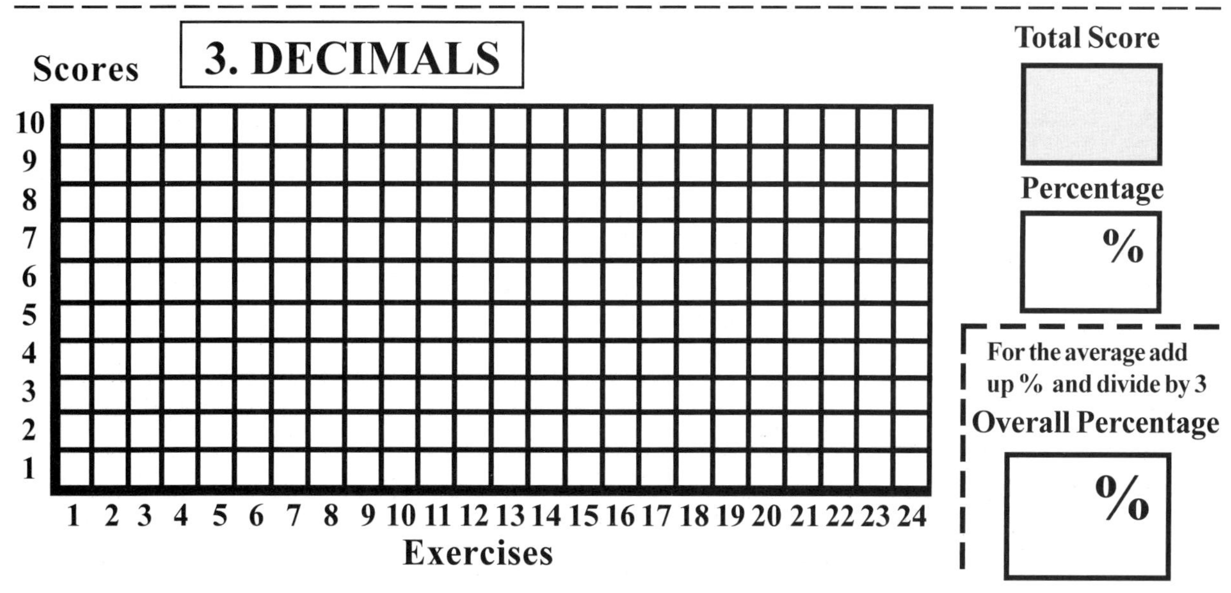

# CERTIFICATE
# OF
# ACHIEVEMENT
## (First)

This certifies............................... has completed **Maths Book One** successfully.

Overall Percentage Score Achieved

%

Comment.......................................

......................................................

Signed ...................................

(Teacher/parent/guardian)

Date ....................